An Overview of ... ... of
... Spirituality

By:

Mignon V. Supnet

Cover Art

By:

Miguel S. Kilantang, Jr.

Text copyright © 2012, 2013 Mignon V. Supnet

Second Edition

All Rights Reserved

This book may not be reproduced or transmitted or stored in whole or in part by any means, including graphic, electronic, or mechanical without the express written consent of the author except in the case of brief quotations embodied in critical articles or reviews.

Table of Contents

Table of Contents 3
Dedication 5
Introduction 6
Chapter 1: What is the difference between Spirituality, Metaphysics, and Religion? 12
    Spirituality 12
    Metaphysics 13
    Religion 14
Chapter 2: Am I on the right track? What's right for me? 19
Chapter 3: What led you here? 24
Chapter 4: What does this all mean? 28
    Angels 31
    Types of Angels or Angel Phylum 32
    Phylum 1--Guardian Angel or Angels 33
    Phylum 2--Archangels 34
    Phylum 3--Cherubim and Seraphim 38
    Phylum 4--The Powers 39
    Phylum 5--The Carrions 40
    Phylum 6--The Virtues 41
    Phylum 7--The Dominions 41
    Phylum 8--The Thrones and Principalities 41
    Chakras 43
    Dreams 46
    Energy 51
    Intuition 54
    Law of Attraction 61

Past Lives 65
Spirit Guides... 71
Chapter 5: Tools and Practices 73
Practice of Breathing.. 73
Attitude of Gratitude 74
Body, Heart, and Mind Awareness 75
Angel Cards.. 81
Reiki 82
Meditation 84
Prayer 86
Visualization... 87
Journaling... 89
Blocking 90
Release 94
Chapter 6: Helpful Terms 97
Chapter 7: Closing 102
Share Your Thoughts 104

Dedication

I dedicate this book to my biggest inspirations in life. It is because of these amazing people that I am who I am today and it is with their love and support that I found the courage to pursue this dream.

My dad, I know you're still watching over me and the family. I hope I'm making you proud.

My mom, you have always been my rock. You are the original and one and only Wonder Woman! You taught me more about God and faith than any church ever has or ever could.

My brother, you have a heart of gold and you shine beyond belief. I've always known you would do incredible things with your life and I'm glad to see that I'm not wrong.

My best buds, Nancy and Alita, you are both beyond words. Nancy, you are my Soul Sister and I am so grateful that I found you. You are the yin to my yang.

Alita, thank you for the laughter. You make the everyday more adventurous and fun. Thank you both for always having my back and I can't wait to see our dreams realized.

And most importantly, my husband and kids, you are my light. It is because of you I know where my home is. My heart is a much bigger and better place because of you.

Introduction

I was raised in a Catholic household. My parents weren't super strict about the religion, but it was important to them that we prayed and believed in God. We went to Sunday mass as much as possible, but there were Sundays when we didn't go to church because of other family plans. If we missed a Sunday, my mom would say that we'd make it up in some other way--like putting more money into the collection basket at the next mass or by saying extra prayers.

I remember Sunday mass was really more of a social event for me rather than a time to devote to God. Often times, Sunday mass would be the only time I could see friends from other schools, or more importantly to see that really cute boy who looked like he was also at church to appease his parents.

While in church I knew when to sit, stand, or kneel. I knew when to join in the prayer verses and when to respond. It was all very automatic really. So automatic in fact that I had no clue why we did what we did and what the prayers truly meant. Half the time I couldn't even understand what the priests were trying to communicate through the gospels they were lecturing on.

I often felt like I was listening to the teacher from the Charlie Brown cartoons. You know the one that sounded like she was droning through a cone, saying wah-wah-wah-wah. Needless to say, I didn't really connect with the religion I was brought up in. When I got older and no longer had to go, I detached from the church completely. I didn't miss it.

Life went on and I thought I was living the ideal life. After all, I did what was expected of me. I finished college, got married, landed a great job, had two great kids, awesome friends… so what could go wrong? Well, life kept going and somewhere along the way, my husband and I separated for two years and nearly divorced; I went through bouts of deep sadness, and then the clincher… my dad was diagnosed with cancer and later lost his life to the disease. My dad died on Mother's Day, May 7, 2009. Little did I know that on that day, my world would start to crack.

I was seven months pregnant with my second son when my dad died. I was a big ball of emotions. There were a lot of days I felt crazy. I was happy one second because I was excited about the arrival of my son and then crying my eyes out the next minute, because my dad wasn't going to be around to meet him.

I was hurting and the pain I had in my heart was like no other I've ever felt before. It was as if someone tore a hole in my heart and left a gap that I could never fill. But I had to move forward. I had to prepare for my son's arrival. There were tons of things to do, things to prepare and get-ready. I got busy. I didn't want to feel the pain. I couldn't take it.

Soon enough, my son was born and our family settled into the routine. I was tired all the time. I started to feel drained and I started to feel heavy emotionally. I thought naturally it's because I'm barely getting any sleep at night. I started to get an awful ache in my chest, but I brushed it off as a side effect of mom-fatigue.

I felt unsettled and restless, but I found a reason for that too. I have two kids now. I'm super busy and feeling pulled in so many different directions. I'm just adjusting to my new role of mom-of-two. I reasoned my way out of my symptoms.

My mom came to stay with us for a couple of weeks to help out with the baby. What a life-saver she was! This was a bittersweet time for my mom and me. We would talk while the baby napped and she would tell me stories about her and Dad, including what it was like for them during his last few weeks. My love and appreciation for my parents grew by leaps and bounds during this time. I couldn't believe the amount of strength, courage, and dignity, my dad possessed. He was in a lot of pain, but not once did he ever act like a victim. Even to his very last days, he remained independent and kept on trying to take care of things around the house.

Then the regret and guilt came. It came rushing at me like the flood gates blew open. I wasn't there for my parents. I lived out of state. I didn't visit enough. I didn't call enough. I didn't help. I wasn't there for them. I was too wrapped up in my own world that even in my parents' greatest time of need, I wasn't there for them. I wasn't there for my dad....

My heart was broken. I didn't think that I could feel any more pain, but guilt and regret have a way of adding to one's misery and sinking an already burdened heart to the lowest depths of the soul.

Before my mom left to go back home, I remember her taking my hands and holding them in hers for a long time before saying *"... you didn't do anything wrong. Your dad loved you and he understood. Let it go."*

Easier said than done. I struggled with my feelings for a long time after my mom left. When I couldn't take it anymore, I started to read. I've always loved books and could always rely on finding the answers I needed in books.

I read everything I could about death and loss, grieving and mourning. You name it, I probably read it. I got to a point where I understood what I was going through. It was normal. There were stages and reasons for why I felt what I felt. OK I got it, but somehow having a cognitive understanding wasn't enough. I was still missing something. I could feel it; it was gnawing at me. My mind was satisfied, but my heart was looking for more. I didn't know what it was, but I had to search for an answer. I went back to books and started looking for different topics about death and loss.

During one of my searches I came upon the subject of past lives. I'd heard about past lives before, but I didn't know much about it. It sounded intriguing so I started to search the web for information on the subject.

I started to read about this concept of past lives and it seemed that the more I read, the more I felt at peace. I felt like I found an answer. I felt like something was opening up in my mind and my heart. I felt comforted by the information I was finding. I didn't feel any resistance to it at all. It made sense to me and I started to accept the information about past lives as my new truth. I came to believe that my dad lives forever and I found comfort in that.

Life went on again and I put my searching on the back burner. I went back to doing my day-to-day routine. Eventually I hit what I call 'my funk.' I was stuck in a rut--a great, big, nasty rut! A rut that felt like life was caving in on me. I've had many of these 'funks' over the years, but it always went away after some time. This one was different. It had a hold on me and wouldn't let go.

I started becoming agitated… edgy. Nothing ever felt right. I felt like I was struggling with everything--even the mundane simple stuff. I felt like a heavy sadness had wrapped around me and I couldn't get away from it. That ache I felt in my chest came back with a vengeance. I couldn't do anything to relieve it. I thought it was a muscular strain so tried to stretch it away--nothing. Exercise it away--zilch. Ignore it away--made it worse. Pray it away--nope still there. I didn't understand what was happening. It wasn't just the physical pain, I felt incredibly lost. I considered therapy. Maybe I needed to be medicated?

I was getting scared and I thought that maybe something was really wrong. Maybe I was sick? But I couldn't tell anybody what was going on. I had just lost my dad and the last thing I needed was for my family to start worrying about me. I didn't want to be a burden on anybody. I've always taken care of things myself and I could handle this too. Problem was I started to feel resentful about everything.

Between the stresses of work and the responsibilities of home, I felt overwhelmed with nowhere to turn. I started blaming my marriage and all the things I thought my husband was lacking and not doing. I started to pray that he would change and at least help out around the house. I mean really, how hard was it to take out the garbage?

My mind dwelled on the negative side of things--including me not being around anymore. Some days my thoughts would be to divorce. Some days I thought what if I was dead? Maybe that would be better. I mean, it's not like I was a great wife and the way I was acting like a madwoman, my kids were afraid of me--even the baby. So many days I felt like screaming, but I kept my mouth shut. I couldn't speak. Hell, there were days I couldn't even think. It was all too much and I felt like I was about to implode.

By this time, not only had the walls of my world cracked, they were beginning to crumble and fall. I felt hopeless and I didn't understand why I was so miserable. To someone looking at my family from the outside, we would have been the "perfect" picture of an ideal family. No one would have seen the fissures that were creeping and getting larger within me.

I wanted peace. I needed peace. My entire being was begging for it. I was confused. I didn't know where this "call for help" was coming from. I had a great life, right? Maybe I do need to be medicated? Did somebody say "Xanax?" What was wrong with me?! I felt like I was going crazy and was about to go over the edge of insanity.

I went back to my books. I started searching the web again, tried finding anything and everything that would help me make sense of my problems. I had this need to understand why I felt so empty.

My spiritual journey began. . .

I am no expert on spirituality or metaphysics, or religion. I am simply a woman who's trying to hold it all together--one step at a time. I have not reached my destination, nor do I expect to reach that place anytime soon. I am in the beginning stages of this voyage, but I feel that I've learned enough to share with you, so you don't feel the same sense of frustration, and of being lost, and of being overwhelmed that I often felt and still feel at times.

I am a work-in-progress just like you. And just like you, I often wanted someone to help me make sense of it all.

Thank you for putting your trust in me and allowing me into your life by reading this book. Although I am no master, I hope to be your travel companion who can provide some assistance and motivation for you to continue your exploration. It is a journey well worth taking and I hope to be of service to you through the lessons I've learned and will share with you throughout this book.

Each of our spiritual paths is different, but we are all somehow connected. I wish you many blessings on your journey, and may you find the truths you seek.

Chapter 1: What is the difference between Spirituality, Metaphysics, and Religion?

First, let's look at the formal definition of each term.

I like to use Wikipedia. You can find information on just about anything on this site. It's very user friendly and offers you other related topics which can make your research more efficient.

According to Wikipedia.org, these are the definitions:

Spirituality

The source below can be found in its complete context here: https://en.wikipedia.org/wiki/Spirituality

There is no single, widely-agreed definition of spirituality.[1][2][note 1] Social scientists have defined spirituality as the search for the sacred, for that which is set apart from the ordinary and worthy of veneration, "a transcendent dimension within human experience...discovered in moments in which the individual questions the meaning of personal existence and attempts to place the self within a broader ontological context."[8]

According to Waaijman, the traditional meaning of spirituality is a process of re-formation which "aims to recover the original shape of man, the image of God. To accomplish this, the re-formation is oriented at a mold, which represents the original shape: in Judaism the Torah, in Christianity Christ, in Buddhism Buddha, in the Islam Muhammad."[note 2] In modern times spirituality has come to mean the internal experience of the individual. It still denotes a process of transformation, but in a context separate from organized religious institutions: "spiritual but not religious."[5] Houtman and Aupers suggest that modern spirituality is a blend of humanistic psychology, mystical and esoteric traditions and eastern religions.[6]

Waaijman points out that "spirituality" is only one term of a range of words which denote the praxis of spirituality.[10] *Some other terms are "Hasidism, contemplation, kabbala, asceticism, mysticism, perfection, devotion and piety".*[10]

Spirituality can be sought not only through traditional organized religions, but also through movements such as <u>liberalism</u>, <u>feminist theology</u>, and <u>green politics</u>. Spirituality is also now associated with <u>mental health</u>, managing <u>substance abuse</u>, <u>marital functioning</u>, <u>parenting</u>, and <u>coping</u>. It has been suggested that spirituality also leads to finding purpose and <u>meaning in life</u>.[3]

Metaphysics

The source below can be found in its complete context here: <u>https://en.wikipedia.org/wiki/Metaphysics</u>

Although the word "metaphysics" goes back to Aristotelean philosophy, Aristotle himself credited earlier philosophers with dealing with metaphysical questions. The first known philosopher, according to <u>Aristotle</u>, is <u>Thales</u> of <u>Miletus</u>, who taught that all things derive from a single first cause or <u>Arche</u>.

Metaphysics as a <u>discipline</u> was a central part of academic inquiry and scholarly education even before the age of <u>Aristotle</u>, who considered it "the Queen of Sciences." Its issues were considered[by whom?] *no less important than the other main formal subjects of <u>physical science</u>, <u>medicine</u>, <u>mathematics</u>, <u>poetics</u> and <u>music</u>. Since the <u>beginning of modern philosophy</u> during the seventeenth century, problems that were not originally considered within the bounds of metaphysics have been added to* its purview, while other problems considered metaphysical for centuries are now typically subjects of their own separate regions in philosophy, such as <u>philosophy of religion</u>, <u>philosophy of mind</u>, <u>philosophy of perception</u>, <u>philosophy of language</u>, and <u>philosophy of science</u>.

Religion

The source below can be found in its complete context here: https://en.wikipedia.org/wiki/Religion

There are numerous definitions of religion and only a few are stated here. The typical dictionary definition of religion refers to a "belief in, or the worship of, a god or gods"[22] or the "service and worship of God or the supernatural".[23] However, writers and scholars have expanded upon the "belief in god" definitions as insufficient to capture the diversity of religious thought and experience.

<u>Edward Burnett Tylor</u> defined religion as "the belief in spiritual beings".[24] He argued, back in 1871, that narrowing the definition to mean the belief in a supreme deity or judgment after death or <u>idolatry</u> and so on, would exclude many peoples from the category of religious, and thus "has the fault of identifying religion rather with particular developments than with the deeper motive which underlies them". He also argued that the belief in spiritual beings exists in all known societies.

The anthropologist <u>Clifford Geertz</u> defined religion as a "system of symbols which acts to establish powerful, pervasive, and long-lasting moods and motivations in men by formulating conceptions of a general order of existence and clothing these conceptions with such an aura of factuality that the moods and motivations seem uniquely realistic.[25] Alluding perhaps to <u>Tylor's</u> "deeper motive", Geertz remarked that "we have very little idea of how, in empirical terms, this particular miracle is accomplished. We just know that it is done, annually, weekly, daily, for some people almost hourly; and we have an enormous ethnographic literature to demonstrate it".[26] The theologian Antoine Vergote also emphasized the "cultural reality" of religion, which he defined as "the entirety of the linguistic expressions, emotions and, actions and signs that refer to a supernatural being or supernatural beings"; he took the term "supernatural" simply to mean whatever transcends the powers of nature or human agency.[27]

The sociologist Durkheim, in his seminal book The Elementary Forms of the Religious Life, defined religion as a "unified system of beliefs and practices relative to sacred things".[28] By sacred things he meant things "set apart and forbidden—beliefs and practices which unite into one single moral community called a Church, all those who adhere to them". Sacred things are not, however, limited to gods or spirits.[note 2] On the contrary, a sacred thing can be "a rock, a tree, a spring, a pebble, a piece of wood, a house, in a word, anything can be sacred".[29] Religious beliefs, myths, dogmas and legends are the representations that express the nature of these sacred things, and the virtues and powers which are attributed to them.[30]

In his book The Varieties of Religious Experience, the psychologist William James defined religion as "the feelings, acts, and experiences of individual men in their solitude, so far as they apprehend themselves to stand in relation to whatever they may consider the divine".[31] By the term "divine" James meant "any object that is godlike, whether it be a concrete deity or not"[32] to which the individual feels impelled to respond with solemnity and gravity.[33]

Echoes of James' and Durkheim's definitions are to be found in the writings of, for example, Frederick Ferré who defined religion as "one's way of valuing most comprehensively and intensively".[34] Similarly, for the theologian Paul Tillich, faith is "the state of being ultimately concerned",[35] which "is itself religion. Religion is the substance, the ground, and the depth of man's spiritual life."[36] Friedrich Schleiermacher in the late 18th century defined religion as *das schlechthinnige Abhängigkeitsgefühl*, commonly translated as "a feeling of absolute dependence".[37] His contemporary Hegel disagreed thoroughly, defining religion as "the Divine Spirit becoming conscious of Himself through the finite spirit."[38]

When religion is seen in terms of "sacred", "divine", intensive "valuing", or "ultimate concern", then it is possible to understand why scientific findings and philosophical criticisms (e.g. Richard Dawkins) do not necessarily disturb its adherents.[39]

Spirituality, metaphysics, religion... oh my! I've always wanted to try a rendition of that! Ok, I digress. It all sounds very official doesn't it? For me it was a little difficult to understand too. I mean how do you define a set of beliefs or a set of principles that is so personal to an individual?

Here's my tip--don't get caught up in the technical terms and trying to understand exactly what each little thing means. That's not what is important. What is important is how you feel about the terms, words, and stories that will be coming to you. What does each thing mean for you? How does it make you feel? Your truths and your meanings will come as you move further in your search. After all this is a journey into discovering yourself and not a science experiment. You don't need to be that precise and do-overs are allowed. It's ok.

Here's what I've learned so far. Here are my definitions.

Spirituality, for me is soul deep. This is the stuff I tap into in times of prayer. It's what gives me hope. It's what gives me faith. I feel this in my heart and it's my internal barometer. It's what kicks in when I'm faced with decisions that require a value judgment. It's what brought me on this path to understand what I'm really about. This is the stuff that makes me tick.

Metaphysics, in my opinion are all the different topics that I've discovered while on this journey. There are multitudes of avenues I've explored. I've studied the Chakra System, Angels, Spirit Guides, Energy, Law of Attraction, etc. Each of these specialty areas has its own version of what is going on with us or with the Universe in general. For example--if you want to know why your relationships are strained, the Chakra System of philosophy may say that it is because one of your chakras is weak and not functioning properly.

Religion, in my opinion is about the structures and rules of an organized church. I was raised as a Catholic and part of growing up within that religion was about the rules and the formality. For me it was also about the lectures that made me feel that God was angry and vengeful. The church taught that if we were not good Catholics, we would end up in Hell and be forever condemned. The rules and formality of the church I accepted because I understood the traditions that they were trying to uphold. I may not have agreed with those rules and traditions, but I understood it nonetheless.

It was this angry and vengeful God concept that I never understood. This idea didn't sit well with me at all. How does a God who made us in his image and likeness, and breathe his own breath into us-- to give us life, also have the capacity to destroy those of us he doesn't approve of?

We are all his children aren't we? I couldn't accept the God that I learned about from the church. There were contradictions and gaps in the lessons and something in my heart told me this wasn't all there was.

I will admit that there were lessons from the church that I took to heart and appreciated learning; but, I felt like I was piecemealing the teachings to get what I needed. That never felt right and I often wondered if there was something more.

My mom would like me to go to church. My mom feels that there is sacredness in going to a House of God to pray. I respect my mom's feelings and perspective and I believe that for her she finds comfort and solace in church. My mom feels connected to God when she prays at church and I support her 100% in this. After all isn't that what we all seek? This connection to our Creator to understand what this world and this life is about?

As you can see, I can't just spout out my definitions in one mechanical description. I'm giving you my meaning based on what my heart is dictating to me. It may not be exactly right according to strict interpretation, but it's what is right for me and you will find what is right for you.

Be patient, slow down, and pay attention to yourself. You'll soon hear your true self speaking--softly, ever so softly at first, but you will hear and when you do, it's time to listen. I will say this: there comes a time when that inner calling no longer whispers and will no longer tolerate being ignored.

That inner calling is your Spirit. Your Spirit is the part of you that is connected to and is a part of God. Your Spirit is the part of you that calls for you to take action and claim your joy, your bliss, and your abundance. It is the real you and your Spirit demands to be heard. This is what this journey is about. It's finding that inner calling, answering it, and releasing the authentic YOU into the world!

As we move along you will find that I prefer to use the term God when I refer to our heavenly creator. This is what I grew up with and how I identify with Him. However, if you are not comfortable with this, feel free to substitute my term for yours. I've seen many references use "Universe", "The Source", "The Creator," "Mother Father God", etc.

Let's get going...

Chapter 2: Am I on the right track? What's right for me?

I can't even count the number of times I have asked these two questions. I grew up learning that I needed approval before moving forward with whatever I was doing. If my parents gave me their permission, then I knew it would be ok and I could keep moving ahead with the confidence that I wasn't screwing up. Then all of a sudden I found myself questioning just about everything I'd learned since I was a kid, and I didn't have anyone to 'give me blessings' anymore.

Ay-yay-yay! What's a woman to do? Everything I had thought was right wasn't so right anymore. I often felt like I was fighting with myself. On one hand I would get so excited about all the new things I was learning because it felt so right, but then on the other hand, there were times I felt my new learning and my new thoughts were sacrilegious!

I would feel guilty for thinking in this new way. I was in conflict a lot of the times. Then I began to slowly realize that I didn't even know what I was about or who I truly was. I found myself asking the greatest question all of all time, "who am I?"

My life had been lived to please other people and to meet other people's expectations--my parents, my husband and kids, my friends, my work, and our community. I did what society and our traditions dictated of me. I lived my role as a wife, as a mom, as a daughter... whatever was expected of me, I did it. I realized that I rarely made any decisions for myself and in the few times that I did, even then, my decisions were based on what I thought other people would approve of. I didn't want to disappoint anybody.

It was a real shock to my system when I recognized that I couldn't live just to please everyone else anymore. What about what I wanted or needed? Did I even know what those were? I hadn't known anything different. My roles were how I functioned. Now what?

My old way of thinking and living was making me feel imprisoned and I wanted to find a way out. Problem was I didn't know how to get out or even which way to turn. I was just frustrated and angry. I felt done! Stick a fork in me, because this turkey was overcooked and dried up!

Wasn't some divine light supposed to shine down on me? Wasn't there supposed to be a choir of angels who would lead me on my path? I had thought that once I turned to God that all these astounding things would happen; that somehow things would just get easier--better. I prayed all the time, so why did I still feel stuck? I felt like nothing was happening. Why wasn't God answering back?

What I didn't realize at the time was that I was getting led and guided. My prayers were being answered. If I had stopped to take notice of what was happening rather than complaining and acting like the victim, then I would have seen what was happening.

Looking back now, I can clearly see that I was constantly being led to materials that I needed in order to learn and understand. I found books, websites, podcasts, and sometimes even songs, yes songs! When it finally dawned on me what was going on, then it became less frustrating and sometimes even fun! You see guidance from God is subtle and a lot of times His answers are not what we might expect, that's why we often fail to see it.

My track initially led me to a lot of different subject matter. I was researching so many things that I felt overwhelmed and confused. One topic would lead to another and then that topic would branch into another. What's right? Who's right? It was information overload and frankly it was aggravating.

Then I stopped. I stopped looking. I stopped searching and I stepped away from the seeking. I didn't pay attention to how long I stopped. It might have been a few days; it might have been a few weeks. I don't remember anymore. What I do remember is that when I went back to searching, it seemed like my searches became more focused. It seemed like I kept looking up the same or similar topic areas. I started to write things down to keep track of them and to this day these are still the same subject areas that continue to fascinate and help me in my day to day life. I'll talk about these topics later in the book.

The more I studied each topic in greater detail, the more I learned, and the more I was able to connect the puzzle pieces that slowly revealed themselves. Think of it this way. You have started on your quest to discover the true meaning of You. If you're just beginning, perhaps you only have a few pavers in front of you that would allow you to move forward. But as you find more information, the more pavers will be set in front of you so that your path continues to grow and extend. Be patient with this. You can't force things to happen. Instead slow down and pay attention to how you're being guided--because you are. Maybe you found this book through that guidance.

How do you know if you're on the right track? How do you know what is right for you? Here's the big answer. You ready? Here it is--you feel it. Yup, that's right... you feel it! The way you feel is so important in this journey. No one knows you like you know yourself. Even if you've lost yourself along the way or if you are like me, who didn't have a true identity, you will know and you will feel what is right for you. That's your Spirit guiding you to your truth.

Here's what I mean. Have you had moments when you're reading a book or listening to the radio and then it feels like the passage you just read or the song that just played was meant especially for you?

Did it resonate with you on some level? Did you feel good about the information? Does something keep popping up "coincidentally" for you? I mentioned earlier that I was even finding information in songs. Sounds crazy, I know, but it happened to me several times. I would be in my car, when all of a sudden a song would come on the radio and there would be a verse or a chorus that would totally answer the question that I've been struggling with. All I could usually do at that time is shake my head, chuckle to myself and say oooh my God!

Two people can be on a spiritual journey at the same time, but it doesn't mean that their destinations or even the paths they take will be exactly the same. The voyage is as unique as the individual. Don't judge your journey or compare it to another's.

My best friend and I, by chance, embarked on our journey around the same time. I feel lucky because I eventually found someone I could talk to and confide in. I was so lost and hurt that I didn't want to talk to anybody. Thank goodness my friend opened up to me and shared her story.

Her story allowed me to open up. Having a friend to talk to relieved the pressure I felt and kept me from losing my marbles. My friend completely understood what I was going through and could relate to the challenges I felt. However, even with this built-in support system in place, I've found that my friend's path is so very different than mine.

There are many occasions when neither one of us can travel down the same road together because she's being called in one direction, while I'm being called to another and that's totally ok. We're each gaining and learning what we need to move ahead in each of our paths.

My friend and I often say that we are *ANAM CARA*--soul sisters and I truly believe we are. We may choose to travel down different paths, but we also find that somewhere down the line, our paths cross again--even if only momentarily. In that crossing we share and we learn from each other until our paths diverge once again.

Here's my tip--if you come upon a topic that really sparks a curiosity within you, follow it and see where it leads! This is where your guidance is telling you to go. There will be something there that will help you make sense of a question you might be asking. Think of this as a spiritual scavenger hunt. You're being given the clues to follow that will lead you to the ultimate prize--the real YOU!

Learn to trust yourself. Heavenly guidance is soft and subtle and there is no negativity attached to it. If you start to second guess yourself, it might be your own negative self-talk that's getting in the way. Go back to your feelings; as long as you are honest with yourself, your feelings will be one of the best tools you have.

Have fun with this! You've chosen and you're on your way! Enjoy the sights to behold as you travel down your chosen road!

Understand that the right to choose your own path is a sacred privilege.

Use it.

Dwell in possibility.

~Oprah Winfrey

Chapter 3: What led you here?

When I started on my spiritual journey, did I know I was going on a journey? Did I, at that time, understand what was ahead of me? Nope. I had no clue.

All I knew was that there was this awful pain in my chest and I was depressed all the time. I had a great need to understand what I was going through. I felt restless and disconnected from my life. I felt such emptiness and I couldn't make sense of it.

Yes, my dad died and I was still mourning his loss, but I knew... I just knew that the darkness and the emptiness I was feeling were from something else. My dad's death triggered something in me. His death was the first blow that cracked my world, but it wasn't the only reason I felt such grief.

I often found myself in a place of darkness--mentally and emotionally. My life felt chaotic and confused and all I wanted was to be away. If I was an ostrich I would have stuck my head in the sand and played blind to the world.

I wanted to find peace for myself. I often thought about my own death. I wasn't suicidal, but I often thought about dying. For me, dying meant going back to God and going back to a place of pure peace and love.

I considered seeing a therapist or a doctor for my problems. But, I didn't. I don't have anything against therapy. I believe therapist and counselors provide a great service, but I knew that it wasn't for me.

What about a doctor, you ask? I never made it into a doctor either. Other than that pain around my heart, I felt physically fine. You're probably thinking, "weren't you scared that something serious was going on? You could've been having a heart attack?!" Believe me the thought crossed my mind and I was scared, but somehow I just knew my issue wasn't medical. I felt like it was something deeper. I knew my problem wasn't going to be solved with medicine or some pill.

I knew that my heart was broken and that's where my pain was coming from.

I didn't know what I was going to do to "fix" myself, but I knew I had to do something. I hated the way I felt, the way I behaved, the way I thought. All in all, I felt like life sucked! Although I remained functional and continued to work and care for my family and our home, it took every ounce of my energy to accomplish anything.

It was so difficult to get through the day--most importantly I worried how my behavior would affect my family--especially my kids. I felt like the worst mother and wife ever. The roles I was playing were no longer enough to sustain me and worse yet, these same roles that I'd carefully crafted over the years were shedding away from me and left me feeling raw.

Then one afternoon, as I was driving myself home from work, I broke down. I couldn't carry the heaviness anymore. I was so tired. I just wanted to stop-- everything. I cried hard, and at that time and in between sobs, I remember saying to God, "I give up. Lord, I give up. I don't care what happens, just take it away." I didn't make any bargains with God, I just asked for my troubles to be gone and I didn't care how He did it. I was done and I didn't know what else to do.

By the time I got home, I noticed that the pain in my chest was much less intense. I also didn't feel so emotionally heavy. What just happened? I was thankful for the relief, but what happened? I've had crying sessions before so what was different about this? And then it hit me! Or maybe it was God that smacked me upside the head and said "duh!"

I surrendered to God. When I felt no more fight left in me, I absolutely and without any hesitation... surrendered. I felt a sense of renewal. Don't get me wrong, I wasn't traipsing through the tulips in that moment, but I felt hope was coming back.

As I look back, I now understand that when I submitted to God, I also let go of the last of the remaining bricks that held my world together. The reality that I knew just got blown to smithereens. My world was in tatters and I had only one choice--to rebuild. I had to rebuild me and find out who I AM.

What was it for you? What rocked your world so much that it made you stop to reassess everything you've been about? Did you also find yourself in a dark place where hope seemed so far out of reach? What finally broke you?

For me it was the loss of my dad that started my quest. For many others the seeking was initiated by something much more positive, but still life changing. I've heard of and have read about many people who've had amazing visions. Visions that were so miraculous that nothing else mattered, but finding the meaning of that vision. And still for others, maybe it was an epiphany that came while they were in the middle of taking a shower or walking the dog!

Whatever happened to you and whether your experience was big or small, good or bad--what matters is that you woke up and you're here now!

Remember that scene in Matrix, when Neo meets Morpheus for the first time? Morpheus offers Neo a choice between two pills. Morpheus explains to Neo that the blue pill would keep him in the world that he knows and there would be no change, BUT, if he took the red pill, he would discover the real world and all illusion would be lifted.

Guess what my friends? You took the red pill! By the way, you'll run into this analogy a lot in your travels through the world of spirituality. It's so fitting don't you think? And much like Neo who discovers his true destiny and is able to pierce through the illusions, you are now also about to discover your purpose... your reality.

Here's my tip--take a moment to reflect back on what got you here. If it was a beautiful experience, embrace it and use that positive feeling to recharge yourself. Smile! Make your whole body smile! Enjoy the feelings of joy and giddiness this brings to you! Revel in the lightness that fills you with this memory.

If it was a painful, traumatic experience, acknowledge what happened and then LET IT GO! That negative experience is now in the past and there isn't anything more you can do about it. Instead, and this may sound crazy, but take a deep breath and then give thanks. You made it through that nastiness and are emerging as an incredible, formidable, and powerful magnificent You!

Recognize where you've been, savor the present, and keep moving ahead.

Yesterday is history, tomorrow is a mystery, today is a gift of God, which is why we call it the present.

~Bil Keane

Chapter 4: What does this all mean?

Our path is getting laid out before us, one paver at a time. Where will it lead?

The possibilities are endless and your spiritual travels will take you to some of the most exotic and sometimes strangest of places you thought possible. This odyssey will take you into yourself more than you've ever known before. You will get to know the many parts of You and what makes you truly special.

The topics I will cover in the following sections of this chapter are what you'll find classified under New Age spirituality and Metaphysics. It's what some of your friends or family may call "airy-fairy spirituality."

In some circles it is not taken seriously and some people may even tell you that this is only a phase you're going through. Please don't let these opinions stop you and your search for truth. The area of spirituality is vast and varied and you may find that you need balance. Your studies may take you from studying ancient Buddhist and Vedic traditions that take you into deep thoughts about existentialism, to the newer studies of spirituality that are more modern and can be supported by science. The more you learn the more comprehension you will gain of your path and why you are searching.

Don't let other people's biases deter you from your path.

When my journey began, I found that the beliefs I had were no longer working for me. I had to reeducate myself and load myself with new knowledge, new ideas, and new theories. Everything that I learned from my Catholic upbringing was falling away. After all my years of going to church and going through several episodes of questioning my belief in God; and not finding the remedies I needed within the church structure to ease my concerns; I lost my faith.

On this journey, I began finding certainties that were so profound that I would be brought to tears. The information would come to me and it felt as if the information was being delivered specifically for me. The veil was being lifted from my eyes and all of a sudden, things started to make sense. The God I used to question was no more. My spiritual path led me to the God I've always believed in and knew in my heart to be true, but I had lost that God because I lost myself.

This journey brought back my faith and solidified my relationship with God. I accept that we are all God's children and we are meant for more. We simply have to claim the gifts that God, the Source, or the Universe, is offering to us. I am thankful every day that my eyes finally opened.

What does this all mean for you?

My hope for you is that you will find what your Spirit seeks. God lives inside of you and by remembering who you really are and waking up to your divine life, you will also know God and his true majesty. I hope that you find the understanding that although you are a unique individual and special in every sense of the word, that you are also an integral part of a much larger whole. You are a part of a divine plan and you have your purpose. You are on this journey now because your Spirit is calling out to you. Your divine spirit wants to be heard and is tired of being in the shadows. It's time to shine and assert your God-given gifts.

The various subjects or topics that I'll cover in this chapter are your resources to help you understand and make sense of the journey you've undertaken. These topics fall under "New Age" studies. Apply the subject areas in your daily life to determine if it is a suitable companion for your journey.

I'll give you a glimpse of the subjects that I gravitated to. There were many other topics I looked into, but these are the ones I've really connected with and where I find peace when I'm trying to understand what is going on with my world.

I encourage you to do your own research. There is an abundance of information available, especially on the internet. What I cover in this book is introductory and meant to whet your appetite. If there is a topic that calls out to you, follow that calling.

Before we proceed, I should warn you that you will find A LOT of information out there. There are many experts on each topic, and guess what? The experts don't always agree with each other. In fact, in some cases they even contradict each other. But don't despair. It's not that one expert is wrong and another is right, it's just each of the experts have found their own personal tweak to a system. The tweak that each expert found happens to be what is working for them. The same will be for you.

Here's my tip--you have to use your feelings to determine what is right for you. Trust yourself. You know when something is right for you. Remember this is YOUR journey and the path that you are traveling on is going to be as unique as you are. If you come across some teachings, techniques, or practice and it feels right for you--go with that. Trust where your internal navigator is sending you. Don't get too caught up in systems or doing things a certain way. You can mix-it-up and really create a customized system of practice(s) for yourself. Many masters and gurus out there apply more than one technique to enhance their spiritual practices.

Follow what feels right with your heart. The more you trust and become aware of yourself, the more you will master what is best for you. You are your own master! Who knows, maybe you'll stumble on the next great practice for seekers like us. The fact of the matter is, if you do the work, you'll know if it's making a difference for you.

Angels

Angels are one of my absolute favorite areas of study. Growing up in a Catholic family, I was familiar with the concept of angels, but I wasn't aware of the true influence and presence that angels have in our lives.

In my childhood home, angels weren't one of the divine bodies that we prayed to, which when I think about it now, is a bit surprising because it seemed like we had a saintly figure that we prayed to for just about every need that might have come up.

Angels are divine beings. They are said to be made of pure energy and are asexual. It is said that the reason we perceive angels as either male or female is because of how we perceive the energy they emanate--meaning one angel could have a more masculine energy versus another who has a more feminine energy. Remember it's about how you feel.

Don't be surprised if you happen to be talking about a particular angel with a friend and your friend perceives that angel as female while you perceive that angel as male. I'll give you an example. Archangel Gabriel. If you were to look up references of Archangel Gabriel in any of the traditional holy texts, Gabriel is referred to as male. However, in current depictions from today's angelologists, Gabriel is female.

It's all good. Both are correct and in my opinion, sex/gender of an angel is not important. What is important are the essence and the message that is associated with the angel and how that angel connects with you.

Angels are a direct manifestation of God and act as God's messengers. Angels are extremely powerful and are sent to us by God to help in our daily lives! Angels can be in many places at once, and because of their energetic form, they can be available to assist--instantly.

There are different types of angels, and I'll briefly go over these, but what they all have in common is that they love us unconditionally and they don't interfere with our free will. This is important to remember; so much so that I'll repeat it again! Angels do not interfere with our free will.

Even when we are being stupid and ridiculous or self-destructive, they let us continue--if that is what we are choosing for ourselves. There's no judgment from the angels that surround each of us--only acceptance and love. Angels understand that we all have lessons to learn and that perhaps it is those lessons that will bring us closer to discovering our true purpose--even if it means they allow us to behave foolishly.

I personally find it comforting to know that with just a thought I could have angelic assistance. Seems crazy huh? But here's the catch, in order to receive angelic assistance, we have to ask! Yes, ask. This is part and parcel of angels not interfering with our free will. The great thing is that angels can and will help us with just about anything. There is no task too great or too small.

Types of Angels or Angel Phylum

Angels have specialties. Even though each group or phylum is all powerful and is capable of great things, each group tends to remain within their scope of expertise. It's comparable to seeking out a doctor. There are many types of doctors and depending on the medical issue you need assistance with, you want to make sure you go to the right specialist. For example, if you're having trouble with your heart, it would be best to seek advice from a cardiologist (heart doctor) and not a podiatrist (foot doctor). Same goes for angels. Each phylum is helpful, but it's probably best to ask for assistance from the right group.

Below, I've listed the eight phyla, or groups of angels. Depending on which book you're reading or website you're researching, there can be up to 10 phyla.

Phyla 1: Guardian Angel or Angels

Phyla 2: Archangels

Phyla 3: Cherubim and Seraphim (sometimes this group is separated)

Phyla 4: The Powers

Phyla 5: The Carrions

Phyla 6: The Virtues

Phyla 7: The Dominions

Phyla 8: The Thrones and Principalities (sometimes this group is separated)

Quick Description of Each Phyla

Phylum 1--Guardian Angel or Angels

Guardian Angel or Angels--I've found some references that say every person is born with at least two guardian angels. These guardian angels are there with us from the time we are born to the time we pass over. They are our constant companion, helpers, and protectors. These angels are the ones that help us stay on our life-path and can call on other resources for help (i.e. Spirit Guides, Archangels, etc.) on our behalf. They literally are our guardians and are ever vigilant.

Have you ever had "near misses" while you're driving? Have you ever wondered how you managed to react so quickly and avoided having a car accident? I've had those too, and many times I'm so shocked and shaken after it happened that I can't even recollect exactly what took place. All I know is that I get a sense of having been saved from what could've been a serious car accident. I truly believe these are instances of my guardian angels' protection and quick thinking.

I also remember a time when I was still a kid. I was sitting outside of my Uncle's home while I was waiting for my parents to come out. There was this man that started walking towards me. We often frequented my Uncle's house, but this man was not somebody I recognized from the neighborhood. I can still remember how angry he looked, and I became more frightened the closer he got. He got to about a foot in front of me and started reaching down towards me, when all of a sudden he started backing away as if shocked by something he saw behind me. He turned, started walking away and went back where he came from.

I remember feeling so relieved when the man left and I immediately said a silent thank you. Shortly after the man left, my parents and Uncle came out chatting happily. I asked if they were just at the door. They said no that they'd been in the kitchen talking.

I've never forgotten this incident and have always wondered what happened to make that man turn away. After learning about angels, I realized that I was saved from that man by my angels. It finally made sense to me and I had one of those a-ha moments. Something terribly bad could have happened to me on that day, but my angels protected me, and I know they continue to protect me now.

Phylum 2--Archangels

Archangels--I personally like to call on Archangels quite often. If you need that extra boost of support, courage, and/or strength for whatever situation you're thinking about--it wouldn't hurt to call on an Archangel's help.

It is said that Archangels' energies are strong and big! I picture these angels to be like those heroic figures, charging through enemy lines while riding on the legendary white steed to save the day! These angels are epic and are probably the most well-known of all the phyla.

The other unique thing about this group is that the Archangels have names. In my research I've found that this seems to be the only group where each angel is individualized or personalized with a name. You'll notice too that most of the archangel names end in "el." The "el" means "in God."

The Archangels are considered healers, but in addition to their healing gifts each one is also a specialist.

Here's my tip--build a relationship with the Angels and Archangels. They are the closest group to us. These angels are the ones with the greatest ability to travel back and forth between the heavens and earth to directly assist us. (The higher the phyla get, the more distance the angel group has from earth. For us this means that the angelic duties that phyla have, is centered more on celestial duties and not earthly ones).

The more you try and connect with your angels and archangels, the more your comfort level will increase. It's just like when you make a new friend. You want to spend time with that person to get to know them and to discover and learn their personality. The Angels and Archangels are our best friends (in waiting) and are always there for us. Get to know them and you'll be better able to see, feel, and/or know the assistance they provide you.

You might be asking "how do you build a relationship with the angels and archangels?" For me, I "talk" to them. Not out loud, but if you wish to have a full-on-talk-out-loud conversation, please go ahead. Again, it's about finding what is comfortable for you. Whenever I have a quiet moment, I try to talk with the angels/archangels. In my head I'm conversing with the angels. Just in case you're wondering if I can hear them answer back...

no, I can't. It's really just me saying my thanks and sometimes going over the events of my day, but I'm directing those thoughts to the angels and archangels. I've found this to be a good way to decompress--especially after a stressful day!

Personally, I think that the angels are the reason I feel better after I have one of my venting sessions. It's like having a friend to listen to every word you say and offering up support just by being there with you and being available.

Here are three of my favorite archangels:

Archangel Michael--is probably the most famous of the archangels. You will find books dedicated to the study of Michael. In the Catholic religion, he is often referred to as St. Michael.

What's cool about Michael is he shows up in all the traditional religions--Catholic, Jewish, Christian, and Islamic teaching. His name means "like unto God."

He is the warrior angel and is often depicted carrying a flaming sword and shield. It is said that it was Michael who led heaven's army against the hordes of Satan and ultimately banished Satan himself.

Michael is an incredible protector and he's there to serve and protect. It's not just about our physical safety; Michael can protect all facets of our lives--family, health, finance, relationships, etc. His energy is so strong that it can supercharge your energy to give you the motivation or the courage you need to move ahead.

If you find yourself in a dark state of emotions, Michael's blazing energy can help pull you through.

Here are some other examples where Michael can help:

~You need strength and courage to try a new venture.

~You'd like extra protection for you and your family.

~You'd like help overcoming fears.

~You'd like help to clear old baggage that might be holding you back.

Of course Michael is not limited to assisting just with these types of issues. He is an awesome angel and can help with any concerns you may be having--no matter how big or how small.

Archangel Raphael--is the doctor amongst the archangels, but unlike human doctors who are limited to addressing only physical and mental injuries, Raphael can heal all. If you need help with physical, emotional, spiritual, chemical, and energetic healing--Raphael is your guy. Raphael's name means "God heals."

I often call on Raphael when my kids get sick. Both of my boys have asthma and I'm thankful that their asthma is well controlled and that on a day-to-day basis, the asthma is pretty negligible. But when the kids catch a cold, then my husband and I are on high-alert and we have to take extra care to make sure that their asthma does not get exacerbated.

For you parents out there who have kids with asthma or any other medical condition, you can understand how stressful and how awful you feel when the kids are ill. I often want to take my kids' 'sick' away or take it on myself so they don't have to suffer through it.

Raphael is a great angel to call on when you, family, or friends are in need of healing--any healing. Raphael can help and he makes house-calls. I've found that when I ask for Raphael's assistance with my kids, I find that their colds are not as severe or last as long. When I call on Dr. Raphael, I find that it's not just the kids that benefit from his assistance; I also get help with my worries and concerns.

Archangel Metatron--Metatron's story is pretty neat. Notice his name doesn't end in "el?" That's because he didn't start out as an angel. He used to be human! Metatron is said to have been the great prophet, Enoch. Enoch was so virtuous in his lifetime that God took him up to the heavens and made him an angel. God gave him great station and made him heaven's scribe to record all of men's deeds. Because Metatron records all of our doings, he basically sees all and knows all. Some resources even say that he sits next to God's throne in heaven.

However, even with his great responsibility, he is still available to help us. Metatron is a great teacher, and because he's been human, he understands the challenges we face. Think of Metatron as your heavenly mentor who can lead you and help you understand your inner calling.

I often call on Metatron when I need assistance with learning new concepts or when I'm starting a new project. I find that with Metatron's help, I am more organized and can formulate a better plan of action to follow.

Phylum 3--Cherubim and Seraphim

Cherubim and Seraphim--I'm sure you've seen a clip in commercials or movies when dark clouds dramatically part to reveal clear, bright, rays of light, shining through the darkness? The scene completes when the darkness dissolves and a heavenly chorus of angelic voices harmonizes an uplifting melody and everyone who hears the music gets bathed in light.

I think the visual is great because this is what I think of when I think about the Cherubim and Seraphim.

The Cherubim and Seraphim are heaven's musicians. These angels are the ones responsible for the heavenly music or the choir that you hear as the dark clouds part to reveal the light.

It seems that the only difference between the Cherubim and Seraphim is how they generate music. The Cherubim use their voice and sing songs to express their love and devotion to God, while the Seraphim produce a musical tone as a means to convey their praise.

The music that is heard from these angels is said to be like nothing on earth--beautiful, moving, but beyond what our limited words could describe.

Angelic music is said to be the type of music that would bring you to your knees from the rush of emotions that will grab you. Music is such powerful medium for communication and many times music can touch upon parts of our Spirit that words cannot.

You might be wondering why singing angels are so important. Ever notice that a lot of prayer verses tell us to sing the praises of God? Although I have not had any personal experiences with this group of angels, I have learned (through research) that in the heavens, these angels sing, not just to sing, but they sing in praise of God. Angelic songs that overflow with love and joy, sung in the glory of God.

When we sing the praises of God as we're taught through prayer; it is these angels that we are emulating.

Phylum 4--The Powers

The Powers--are also healers like the Archangels. Where they differ is how they heal. Archangels will use tools like a scepter to send you the healing energy you need while, the Powers will wrap you within their wings and envelope you in healing energy.

The first time I went to a Reiki session, I had a vision that I came upon a great big angel. As I came upon the angel, the angel hugged me and his wings closed around me. I felt very comforted and loved and I didn't want to let go, but the vision started to fade.

I think about this experience a lot because I don't have visions. This seems to have been a one-time event. I've returned for additional Reiki sessions, but I haven't had that vision again or any other vision for that matter. That makes that experience even more special to me and when I recall the vision in my mind, I can still feel the comfort and love that I felt. I believe that great big angel I saw during my Reiki session is one of the Powers.

Phylum 5--The Carrions

The Carrions--these angels (to me) are very mysterious. These angels are definitely protectors, but in a very distinctive way. Carrions are the angels that make sure that dark spirits or dark energies don't linger on earth after the dark spirit dies. These angels are the ones charged with escorting the dark beings away from earth and away from us.

Can you imagine the chaos that could happen if it weren't for this group of angels who ensure the dark spirits' passage? I know this seems far-out doesn't it? I think what was more surprising to me when I learned about these angels were not so much the existence of this group of angels, but that there are dark beings present. I guess in my naïve nature, I thought dark spirits were only stuff of movies.

Remember when I told you, that some of the things that you will come upon during your exploration will be exotic and strange? For me this was one.

Phylum 6--The Virtues

The Virtues--these are the angels that are in charge of our life charts. Our life chart is like our roadmap to get us to our life purpose. Life charts are created before we are born. (We'll talk more about life charts more when we get to Past Lives.)

Phylum 7--The Dominions

The Dominions--these angels are the record keepers and are the ones keeping track of all of our good deeds.

When I was growing up, there was an often recited story, of a person going to heaven. While that person is at the Pearly Gates, St. Peter comes out and pulls out a list. This list contains the names of the people who can enter the heavenly gates. Along with the names are the deeds that person has done during their lifetime.

How does the story end? If the person has a lot of good deeds they get to enter, no good deeds, they go where it's very hot.

After learning about the angels, I've come to realize that it is The Dominions who basically put together St. Peter's list and officially records it within the Akashic Records. (More on Akashic Records later in the book.)

Phylum 8--The Thrones and Principalities

The Thrones and Principalities--this is the highest level of angel phylum. These two groups are the closest to God. In fact these are Mother-Father God's armies.

Let me explain the concept of Mother-Father God. This is still God or the Universe or the Source, or the Creator. They are all one in the same. The term Mother-Father God comes from the notion that God has both male and female aspects. Not that God is two separate beings. God IS. God is everywhere. God is Presence. And God is perfect and whole in his oneness.

Mother-God refers to the god aspects of femininity or the divine feminine--qualities like nurturing, gentleness, and compassion. While the Father-God refers to the god aspects of masculinity--qualities like constancy, protectiveness, and strength. This dual aspect is also reflective of us--his children. We too have both masculine and feminine qualities about us, yet we are one whole person.

The Thrones belong to Mother-God aspect and are said to protect the world from darkness. These angels are dispatched in times of imminent danger. The Principalities belong to Father- God aspect and are said to protect the very nature of spirituality and religion itself. Both Thrones and Principalities protect the masses in times of greatest need.

This concludes the Angels section. Each of these groups of angels can offer support whenever needed. If you don't know which group to call on, no problem, and no worries; just ask for the help and the angels will find the right resource for you. It can be very magical if you allow angelic help to come into your life.

Don't hesitate to ask for help from the angels. They are immensely powerful and want to help us--we just have to ask for it.

Angels have no philosophy but love.

~Terri Guillemets

Chakras

Chakra comes from Vedic studies. In Sanskrit, chakra means "wheel." Each person has seven chakras. The chakras are lined up along our spine--from the base of the spine all the way to the top of our heads. Each chakra has influence over a specific physical, emotional, and/or spiritual process. It is through our chakras that we are able to connect to our spiritual self.

Think of your chakras as the doors to the spiritual world. Chakras are where spiritual energies are stored and collected. You want these doors to be open and receiving of the Universe's guidance.

Here's a quick table to help you reference the chakras:

Chakra	Color	Location	Influence
1	Red	Base of spine	Grounding
2	Orange	Sacral-pelvic area	Creative energy
3	Yellow	Solar Plexus-'gut'	Personal power
4	Green	Heart	Emotions/love
5	Blue	Throat	Expression of truth
6	Indigo	Third Eye-between eyes	Clarity, intuition
7	Violet	Crown-top of head	Oneness with God

Chakras develop at different times, meaning each chakra has a time when it becomes active within our body. Depending on what particular life experience we may be having at the time a specific chakra is coming on, that chakra's development could be enhanced or impeded.

There are tons of resources on the chakra system. What's great about the chakra system is that it can be applied to just about anything, in fact the chakra system can work great when you partner it up with another tool or practice.

Here are some examples of how the study of chakras is usually partnered with another practice:

~Meditation, to strengthen or cleanse a specific chakra (or all of them).

~Yoga and chakra. Yoga can help open up the chakras through certain poses and in combination with breathing exercises.

~Healing stones and chakra. Healing stones can help you feel better connected to your chakras. Healing stones can enhance the healing and/or flow of a chakra.

When all of our chakras are working, we are in the flow and feel one with the Universe. Things are easier, less stressful, and we are more authentic. This is the goal right? Yes it is!

As for me, I'm still working on it and I'm finding out that my challenges tend to be centered on the same chakras.

You might find that you are really strong in certain areas of your life, while you might have more struggles in another. This could be that the chakra that is influencing that part of your life is not working like it should. That chakra could be blocked or is weak or maybe even closed. The good news is that there are techniques available that can help with relieving your chakra ailment.

I've tried chakra meditations. I've found some meditation podcasts on iTunes that have been pretty good. I do have to confess that I am still working on my meditating abilities. I tend to have a lot of mind chatter and meditating is difficult for me. If this is the same for you, try meditating in short spans. I can usually quiet my mind for a solid minute or two before the mind chatter comes back.

Believe it or not, one minute is progress. If you find yourself in this same situation, don't give up. Anytime you can quiet your mind, even if it is only for a few seconds, that is still time you are allowing yourself a quiet space.

I happen to like asking the Angels for help with my chakra healing. I feel that the angels know which chakra needs work. What I've also found very helpful for my chakras is going to a Reiki practitioner. I've mentioned Reiki a couple of times now and I'll give you more details about Reiki later in the book.

Find what works for you in how you connect with your chakras. Connecting with your chakras can be beneficial by allowing you to connect with your Spirit self. Your connection to your chakras could mean that you become more comfortable and accepting of your personal power, or of your intuitive abilities. Connecting with your chakras, can also be very healing by allowing you to release blocks which can be in the form of past and current hurts.

Releasing old wounds or negative energy is a huge exercise in spirituality and using one or several chakra therapies can help with the process of release.

Having basic knowledge of what the chakras are and what they do is helpful. You'll find a lot of reference to the chakra system embedded within many other subjects. In my opinion many spiritual followers see the chakra system as an integral part of our being. We and our chakras are inseparable. It's a part of who we are.

Take for example our physiological body systems (circulatory, digestive, neuromuscular, etc.); although we don't need to intimately understand the complexities of how each of these systems work, we do need to acknowledge that our body systems are vital in our ability to stay physically well and healthy. This same philosophy of acknowledging the chakra system's importance to our spiritual wellness is fundamental in our ability to maintain or facilitate spiritual health.

Dreams

This topic is very intriguing, but can be very complex. The cool thing about dreaming is that there are no special skills required to dream. Everyone dreams. Dreaming is a built in ability we all have.

Our sleeping minds are very open. The normal barriers we have during our conscious hours are down during sleep. This is important because part of what allows us to get in touch with Spirit or the spiritual realm is openness and allowing for the connections with Source to happen.

Dreams may be the way we receive the information from the Universe and how our physical brain interprets the information from the Universe.

There are different states of sleep when our dreams start to occur. If you decide you want to learn more about the science of dreaming, you'll come across these terms:

Sleep Cycle

NREM (Non Rapid Eye Movement). During this phase of sleep, we are not dreaming. We are very still, and our heart rate as well as our breathing is slow and steady. There are four stages of NREM sleep with each stage taking the sleeper, deeper and deeper into sleep until they reach REM sleep.

REM (Rapid Eye Movement). REM is when dreams start to happen. During this phase of sleep we are anything but still. Our muscles twitch, our breathing becomes irregular and even our heart rate can go up.

Have you ever had a dream where you were running? All of sudden you wake up and you're still breathing hard? You were in REM sleep and your body was experiencing in real time, the events you were going through in your dream.

Dreams have been studied for many years. The most famous scientist who brought dreaming to the forefront and gave it recognition amongst modern society is... yes, you guessed it... good old Dr. Sigmund Freud. If I had to make a bet, I would say dreams and dreaming gained popularity because much of Dr. Freud's associations with dreams have to do with sexual matters. After all, sex sells right?

However, using dreams as a sort of tool to understand our own plight or that of our community has been around forever. Dreaming is probably one of the oldest if not the oldest way of communing with the divine. Dr. Freud was not the first to interpret dreams; in fact, shamans from all cultures practice some type of dream communion; the ancient Greeks had the Oracles to make predictions, and Buddhist monks regard dreaming as a way to release oneself from the physical body and release the inner spirit to gain an understanding of one's life path.

There are different kinds of dreams: daydreams, regular dreams, lucid dreams, and nightmares. For our purposes, I'm going to talk about lucid dreams. Lucid dreaming is when you basically know that you're dreaming. For those who have gained further skills in dreaming, they can even control their dreams during a lucid dream state.

Lucid dreaming is a popular area of study for seekers like us because it is in this type of dreaming where we have the most opportunity to gain knowledge from the Universe. It is within this realm of dreaming where we can enhance our dream skills as well as gain an understanding of what our dreams mean. Dreams can be a valuable tool in providing insight to our Spirit's calling. The trick is figuring out what our dreams are trying to tell us.

A dream can have one of three purposes:

~A dream can be a form of communication from the spiritual realm.

~A dream can be prophetic.

~A dream can be our mind's way of sorting out the day or the stress we've been dealing with. I call this mind-chatter dreaming.

Dream interpretation can both be fun and wearisome. I don't know about you, but my dreams tend to be on the weird side. I rarely have a dream when things are normal in the dream. My dreams usually have some element of strangeness to it--my dreamscape is quite surreal.

If I'm lucky enough to remember my dream when I wake up, I will use dream interpretation websites to help me figure out my dream. Mostly I do this for fun and I take the interpretation with a grain of salt. More often than not, the dream symbols that the interpretation provides do not connect with me.

Here's my tip--if you're trying to figure out what your dreams mean, go with the feeling you have when you first wake up. Especially if you were lucid dreaming, you know what you were doing in that dream. Go with the feeling that you're left with after you've woken up. Sometimes the feeling could be faint, but you'll have a sense of what it is. Keep that feeling in mind. Write it down. If the meaning doesn't hit you right then and there, it will come to you later. Your interpretation of your feeling will be more accurate than any meaning a website can give you.

One of the hardest things to decipher is what type of dream you're having--communication, prophetic, or mind-chatter. Don't worry about the type, but rather focus again on the feeling that you're left with and trust it. Pay special close attention to those dreams that stick with you so strongly that thinking about the dream causes an emotional rise in you. The more you pay attention to your dreams and become aware of your feelings, the more you will know the significance of what a particular dream may have for you.

It was about two weeks before my dad passed away when I woke up from a dream crying uncontrollably. I knew I was dreaming about my dad, but I couldn't remember the details of the dream. All I could feel was this extreme sadness centered on my dad and I knew something was wrong. I could not stop crying. The next day, I got a call from my mom that dad was not doing well and that I needed to go home and visit right away.

This dream was a communication dream. After my dad passed away, I confided in my mom about this dream and she felt that it was actually my dad trying to communicate to me.

I had another dream that my brother and I got into a huge argument. I don't remember what the topic of argument was about, only that the verbal fight was heated and emotional.

I remember waking up feeling so upset that I was on the verge of tears. It took me several minutes to actually realize that it was a dream I was coming out of and not an actual fight with my brother. This dream bothered me for days. I don't have fights with my brother. We're very close and often agree on many things. We're also both easy-going people. Getting into such an escalated confrontation would be unthinkable for us.

I thought that maybe it was just my own stress and worries that was somehow manifesting itself into my dreams. I minimized the intensity of the feelings I had when I woke up from the dream and decided that the dream was probably just mind-chatter.

Well, lo' and behold! It was about two months after I had the dream that my brother and I got into a huge and emotionally driven argument. After I caught my breath, calmed down, and talked with my brother like a sane person, the memory of the dream came rushing back at me! The feelings were exactly the same! It was almost like having a deja-vu moment. Oh my God! I had a prophetic dream and didn't know it till it happened!

Additional tips--one of the biggest challenges to dream interpretation is remembering the dream. Here are some things I've tried and have found helpful:

1) Before you sleep, ask for help remembering your dreams. Ask God or ask the angels to help you remember your dreams. God wants us to grow and find our true calling. Our prayers ARE answered all the time. If dream recall is what you are asking help with, God will provide you with the best help there is--his Angels. Remember the angels can help with anything. Shoot, if you're lucky, an angel could even show up in your dreams.

2) I happen to really like sleeping. It's one of my favorite past-times. I don't like having my sleep interrupted to write down a dream in the middle of the night. So I don't. Instead, when I am ready to wake up and if I happen to be waking up from a dream, then that is when I jot things down. A lot of dream experts will probably "tsk-tsk" my method because I'm not capturing the dream as they occur, but I'm ok with that. I'm comfortable with trying to figure out my dreams with the bits that I do have. You'd be surprised how much you can still figure out with the bits. Do what is comfortable for you. Not into writing? Try a voice recorder. Most smart phones have this application available.

3) If you are going to write down your dreams, really write them down. This is why I like to do it when I'm waking up because I can take the time to write. When you write, just start writing and don't worry about sentences, syntax, format, spelling, nothing. Just write. Write down what comes to you for as long as the information is flowing into you. When you're done, set down

your notes and come back to it later. When you come back to it later, something will strike you--it could be that you remember more of the dream, or maybe you will remember a symbol within the dream or the meaning will suddenly hit you. Use this same type of process if you decide to voice record. Just talk and speak the first things that come to you. Again, no edits, no re-do, just talk.

Take the time to pay attention to your dreams and discern what is being communicated to you by the Universe and what your mind is simply trying to work out on its own to release some stress.

With some practice and some effort, your world of dreams can be where Spirit shows you that the impossible becomes possible. That there are no limits; except for the ones we create. Dreaming can be the first step to creating your reality. Your Spirit, through the vessel of your dreams could be urging you to live big, live happy, and let yourself go free. Isn't it worth finding out?

Don't limit yourself and see how your world changes for the better.

All our dreams can come true, if we have the courage to pursue them.

~Walt Disney

Energy

Everything is energy. You will hear this A LOT! Many of the theories surrounding spirituality and metaphysics are centered on this core idea. We are all energy, including the inanimate objects that are around us. We are all particles of energy that vibrate at certain speeds, strength, and waves.

What's cool about this, especially for those of us science fans, is that this theory is based on quantum physics. In physics, a quantum is the smallest quantity of a physical property and quantum physics is the science that studies these smallest measures of property--energy.

Quantum physics is totally legit and a well-respected branch of science. What is difficult for most new seekers is that the world of spirituality is intangible. For those of us who live in modernized western societies, it becomes even more difficult because our focus is only on the material.

We do not accept what we cannot explain with logic. We have been trained to think and to prove, to have data and facts that can be substantiated with science. If we cannot prove something or find evidence, then it must not be real. We have been trained to be analytical and to make our decisions based on a cognitive analysis of a situation.

The study of energy as it relates to science is tangible. Energy experiments show that energy can be harnessed, utilized, and measured. Energy is a fact and not just a concept. Energy studies are supported with hard evidence that can be predicted and replicated over and over again. Prediction and replication are the golden measures in science and it is these same measures that allow scientists to support and prove a theory.

So how does energy relate to spirituality? We are energy beings. Our Spirit, our life force is energy. We are energy in an embodied form. Our bodies although solid, if broken down to the most basic of parts would reveal a collection of atoms which are basically made up of both positive and negative particles of energy. We are one big sack of atoms with all of our physical parts and all of our spiritual-energetic parts vibrating and pulsing at specified frequencies, waves, and lengths of energetic force.

This energetic force that we are made of is what travels to connect with the universal consciousness. It is through this energy that we create our world. How you may ask? Your thoughts, your feelings, and your actions are all forms of energy. Whatever you do causes a ripple effect in your world. Some of the effects may be obvious while others are not. It's like throwing a stone in a pond. That one little drop that the stone creates in the water will create waves that will travel all the way to the edges of the pond. Those waves touch everything that it passes through--those on top of the water and even those underneath the water's surface. Same goes for us. Our thoughts, our feelings, our actions like the stone dropped in the water, will have an effect on us and our world in general.

Here's an example. Have you ever had an occasion when you were thinking about somebody and then that person calls you as if by magic? This happens to my mom and me a lot. I would call her and she would immediately say, "I was just thinking about you." This is energy at work. We are all connected to each other through our energies and when energetic frequencies are aimed at you through thoughts or emotions, you will get the message subconsciously and it will cause you to react in some way.

Let's go back to our atomic studies in high school. Remember protons, neutrons, and electrons? The protons have a positive charge, the neutrons are neutral, and the electrons have a negative charge. Remember how the basic atomic model was depicted? The protons and the neutrons are clustered together in the middle, while the electrons spin around at the outside perimeter of the proton/neutron cluster? There is a natural invisible force that separates the positive proton/neutron cluster from the negative electron.

What's my point for agonizing you with this? This is where science and spirituality meet and work together. In both areas of study, scientists and spiritual masters agree that positive and negative energy repel each other. This is a fundamental universal law that goes to the very building blocks of our beings.

If you are vibrating at a positive level and a person coming up to you is vibrating at a negative level, you will feel it. The energy fields from each person will repulse each other naturally because there is a discord in the frequencies of energy. What is the physical result you feel? You get uncomfortable, you get stressed, and in some cases, you might just want to leave to get yourself away.

But on a positive note, if you come across someone or something, like an event that is in accord with your own vibrations, you will feel good. You will feel light, happy, or excited because you are being surrounded in energy that is vibrating and humming at the same frequencies as yours. You are in resonance with the energy. You feel connected because you are connected. You are plugged in, so to speak.

Here's my tip--the only thing you have to remember about energy is this:

>*Positive attracts positive. Negative attracts negative.*

Intuition

Intuitions are like dreams. It's built into us. We all have it and we can all use it. There's not a whole lot of extra effort involved. Our intuition is always working. However, as our society has moved closer to science and technology where proof and evidence are relied upon, we have lost or maybe more accurately--forgotten our intuitive nature.

We are born with intuitive gifts. Every single one of us--doesn't matter who. We are all intuitive. However, with our societal programming, we haven't learned to use this innate power. I think this is partly why we struggle so much because we are not using all of our God given senses.

Have you ever had an experience where you had to make a choice? One choice seemed "crazy" or "outlandish", but this choice felt really good to you. You had a "gut feeling" about that choice, but because that option was deemed not practical by your friends or maybe because your family did not approve of it; you second-guessed yourself and went against your gut?

Then what happened? Your gut intuition panned out. Had you taken that "crazy" choice, it would have resulted in something awesome--extra money, a great investment, a new job, a new relationship, but none of it happened because you didn't follow your gut.

How often have you said "Aargh, I knew it! I knew if I did (*fill in the blank*), it would have been great!" But more often than not, it's the regret of not following our instincts that we experience rather than the excitement of reaping the great results from following our intuition.

That gut feeling is your intuition at work. It's that part of you that is most sensitive to the calling of God and your Spirit. It's your connection to the invisible world of the divine. I'm sure you've heard of the sixth sense? The sixth sense refers to our intuition. Much like our sense of touch, taste, hearing, smelling, and sight; our intuition also serves to guide us and allows us to better navigate the world around us.

There are different kinds of intuitive senses. While everyone has at least one of these abilities inherent to their person, there are others who could have multiple "clairs" working for them.

What are the "clairs?" For our purposes here, I will only discuss the most common of the "clairs."

~Clairvoyance (clear seeing)

~Clairaudience (clear hearing)

~Claircognizance (clear knowing)

~Clairsentience (clear feeling/sensing)

Clairvoyance

Clairvoyance is having the ability to see into the unseen world of spirit. This type of seeing is not done with the physical eyes, but rather the third-eye. It is this skill that people refer to when they say they've had a vision.

One clairvoyant's skill will differ from another's. There doesn't appear to be a cookie-cutter recipe for this skill. It's as varied as the people who possess them. For example, some clairvoyant intuitives are very good at seeing another person's aura or energy field. This skill can be so strong in fact that they could diagnose a person's life issue based on how the aura is being displayed.

Another clairvoyant could have skills in seeing past-lives or perhaps of seeing future events. Or another could be strong in seeing angels and guides. There are many ways to *see*; how the skill develops from one person to the next will likely differ in part due to the individual's natural strengths and predispositions.

My friend has visions. There have been several times when we're in the middle of a conversation or an activity and she will have "flashes." We work together and park in the same city garage. I remember there was one time when I was pulling into my parking spot and my friend was waiting for me by her car. I noticed that she was hesitating and not wanting to come up to my car like she normally does. When I got out and started walking towards her, she asked "what happened to your friend?" I looked at her puzzled and asked "what friend?"

She explained that she didn't want to come up to me right away because she noticed that I had someone in the car with me and that it seemed like we were having a fun conversation because my friend/passenger had a big smile on her face. I looked at my friend and told her that I didn't have anyone with me and if she was sure she saw someone. She said without a doubt--yes. We started talking about it more and she described to me what she saw and the feeling that she got while she watched us.

By the time we walked into our office, my friend came to the conclusion that she must have seen one of my guardian angels. My friend's vision was especially significant for me because just before I got to the garage, I'd been thinking about a decision I needed to make and I asked the angels to give me a sign if my decision was in alignment with my greatest good.

I did not tell my friend about my request for a sign from the angels and there was no way she could have known. The positive feeling that my friend conveyed to me along with the vision of my angel was my confirmation that I was on the right track.

Clairaudience

Clairaudience is the ability to hear the world of spirit or of the divine. Clairaudient intuitives can hear whispers or maybe full force regalia, when the Universe wants to make a point. The messages could be from angels, spirit guides, passed loved ones, or maybe even the individual's own Spirit self.

You might be able to relate to this in this way; have you ever had a song stuck in your head? No one else can hear the song, but in your mind, you clearly hear the song's melody, lyrics, and chorus; so much so that you eventually start to sing or hum the song. This is similar to a clairaudient experience. The message is being heard inside your mind rather than the message being received through the physical ears.

Hearing voices sounds unnerving and this is probably why people with this gift tend not to reveal their ability. Our society has not yet accepted that we as people are so much more than our physical bodies. We are Spirit, we are energy, and we are all interconnected through a web of energy with the Universe.

Being guided through a clairaudient experience is about hearing messages from Spirit. This means that the guidance is always positive and never negative. If you find that you are hearing that little voice in your head, but the voice is causing you to second guess yourself, or cause you worry, or concern, this voice is likely that of your ego.

Your ego is that part of your mind that likes to be in control and is not receptive to change. This is the part of your mind that is entrenched in the physical world and carries all of your life's programming. The ego wants to preserve and protect you, but often times; the ego does so through fear and doubt.

Claircognizance

Claircognizance is about having a knowing, a certainty of something that you know to be true. Of the "clair" abilities, this is the one I resonate with the most. In my opinion, it is also the skill that can be overlooked and regarded as natural.

When I started my journey I often prayed for a skill to make my journey easier. I thought things would be so much better if I could *see* or *hear* what direction I should be taking rather than fumbling my way around.

I can tell you that I don't have visions and I can't hear divine advice. But do you remember when I said that our prayers are always answered? For me, I usually find my answers in books and during my asking I was led to a book that made me realize that my prayers were answered. I do have a gift. I have claircognizance or at least the budding beginnings of one. I am still developing my skill, but when I have those moments of clarity--it is undeniable.

The reason I say this skill can be overlooked is because there is nothing paranormal or weird in how it shows itself. For me, I've always been drawn to books and I'm always trying to learn and understand the "whys" of the world.

I read a lot and books are a constant in my life. Even before my spiritual quest, I was always on the search for information. I love history and the study of ancient cultures and rituals. I've always had a fascination with magic, fantastical creatures and sacred locations like Stonehenge and the Great Egyptian Pyramids.

Because I do read so much, when a question came up and I knew the answer to it, I simply thought that it must have been because I've read about the topic before. That's what I thought, anyway.

After reading *Discover your Psychic Type, by Sherrie Dillard*, I realized that everything, I was naturally drawn to, like books and the need to understand, is an innate characteristic of a claircognizant. Now that I am aware of this, I have made it a point to take notice of those moments when I just seem to know, without knowing how I know.

My husband was very ill during the fall of 2011. He required emergency care and we ultimately found out that he had a tumor in his stomach. Hearing the word tumor and cancer were devastating to me. I had lost my dad to cancer just a few years before and I couldn't bear to think that I could possibly lose my husband too.

I had to hold it together; I had to keep my thinking clear. There was so much information coming from the doctors. Tests had to be completed, consults needed to be arranged, appointments needed to be kept. I had to stay on top of it all and still maintain some type of normalcy for the kids.

I prayed and I prayed and I prayed some more. I was scared and I couldn't help, but think of worst case scenarios. There were some nights that I fell asleep while praying. I needed God to hear me on this. I was not ready to lose another person that I love. I could not survive my heart being broken again. I prayed and pleaded for my husband's health and for our family's future.

When it came time to make a decision about surgery, my husband and I decided as partners; it was mutual and there was no looking back--surgery had to be done. Surgery day came and while I sat in the hospital waiting room, waiting for my husband to get out, a knowing came over me that everything was going to be ok. My nerves settled down and I felt warmth and calmness spread through me. I think I even smiled.

When surgery finished and the doctor came out to tell me and the family that everything went well, for me it was confirmation (of that *knowing*) that EVERYTHING would be ok. My prayers were answered. Yes, there was going to be post-surgical recovery and chemo treatments, but I knew deep in my heart that all was well. This knowing was not wishful thinking. I knew. My entire being knew as fact that my husband would be ok.

I am happy to say that I was right. My husband continues to do well and our family is thriving.

Clairsentience

Clairsentience is having the ability to clearly feel other people's feelings. It's having that emphatic ability of understanding another person's feelings; but also having the ability to feel those feelings as if they were your own.

I truly feel that most people are natural empaths. It's how we're able to relate to one another and feel what another person must be going through especially in times of distress. It's how we find compassion and understanding for each other.

Clairsentient intuitives feel the feelings of another person in much greater magnitude. They feel the emotions to the same level and ferocity as the person who is feeling the feelings. This skill can be very troublesome in that it can be difficult to separate the feelings of another from the feelings of the intuitive.

Have you ever been with a person who is a downer? That person who always has something bad to say about somebody else. They're never happy about anything and they always seem to have a dark cloud hanging over them. Yeah, we all know at least one person like that.

After you've spent time talking with Mr. or Ms. Doom-and-Gloom, don't you feel tired and perhaps even in a bad mood yourself? Do you feel drained of your energy after being around people like this? Just a word of caution, you might be clairsentient and if you are, that means you will be very sensitive to other people's energies.

There are additional "clair" abilities, but I've only discussed the most common ones here. If this area of study is of interest to you, I would highly recommend reading *Discover Your Psychic Type by Sherrie Dillard*. This book will offer you more details on each "clair" as well as provide you quizzes to determine which "clair" ability you are most predisposed to.

Here's my tip--discovering that you have one or many of these abilities can be confusing. Especially if this isn't the kind of experience you've been exposed to before. Remember, being intuitive is a natural ability we all have.

Your gift is a part of who you are. If your awakening has also awakened your gifts--this is a good thing. These gifts are meant to be helpful. Whichever of the "clairs" you find yourself having, practice it, develop it and do not be afraid of it.

You have a God given talent that will enable you to live a richer, more connected life. Embracing your gifts and talents and claiming them as your own will be a part of your spiritual journey. Dare to discover your strengths through your intuition. You will love who you find.

Law of Attraction

Law of Attraction is a huge topic. Everyone is interested in this because it has the potential to bring you your heart's desire. Your wildest dreams come true.

The Law of Attraction is based on the study of energy and that we are all energy beings. Our thoughts and our feelings go out into the universe as energy.

The Law of Attraction is based on the principle that like attracts like, and while this is true, what most people fail to recognize is that this attraction can also include the negative stuff.

The Universe does not judge our thoughts and our feelings. It simply wants to deliver what we ask for. In order for the Law of Attraction to work, we must make an effort to change the kind of energy we put out. Remember positive attracts positive and negative attracts negative.

In order to put the Law of Attraction to work correctly, here are some basic things to keep in mind:

~Be in a positive state of energy. Have positive thoughts and positive feelings about what you are asking for and about life in general.

~Be clear about what you are asking for. See this clearly in your mind.

~Believe and trust that you will be answered.

The Law of Attraction seems simple enough doesn't it? It's almost like finding the proverbial genie in a magic lamp. "Make a wish and it shall come true, says the Genie." However, the Genie does not tell you that there are caveats to this command.

Here they are:

~You can attract the negative.

~Your subconscious thoughts have strong energetic vibrations and it is the stuff in your subconscious that the Universe picks up on first.

Here's an example and probably one of the most common wishes for the Law of Attraction. You want to attract money because you want to pay off your bills. However, because the bills are such a source of stress for you, every time you get a bill in the mail, you get a strong physical and emotional reaction to the bill and it ruins your day.

In that moment you may be thinking how great it would be to have the money to pay for the bill, and you pray for the money to come. You think positive thoughts about money and know exactly how the money will help you and how the money will help improve your life. However, what you may not be aware of is that your subconscious thoughts don't believe you!

While you may be actively thinking happy thoughts about money, your subconscious is thinking how terrible the bills are and how you have no money because everything is going to your bills and how you will always be struggling with your finances.

Your subconscious thought is stuck in negativity and continues to think that bills are bad and you have no money, no money, no money! Because your subconscious mind is so powerful, it is the energy of the subconscious that is getting transmitted to the Universe.

So, what comes next? More bills and no money! The Universe delivered to you what you felt most strongly about. You felt strongly about the bills so you got more bills. You felt strongly about having no money, so you got no money.

Your subconscious mind requires retraining, unblocking, and/or re-programming. For example, an exercise you might try to retrain your mind, is to see the bill through a different set of eyes. Instead of the bill being a money-sucking monster intent on taking all of your funds and causing you stress and fear about your finances; see the bill as a symbol of your independence. *(You can change this analogy to suit whatever works for you.)* Let the bill empower you and bring you feelings of confidence and assurance. If it is a utility bill, use that bill as a symbol of your comfort--you have heat, air, and running water to make your life easier. The bill is your friend.

This isn't an easy task to do and it will take work. Frankly, you might even laugh at yourself the first time, you thank your bill. I did! Your conscious mind will make you feel silly, but keep at it and eventually those bills won't feel so ominous.

Your subconscious mind is tough to crack. It is called subconscious for a reason; it is beyond our active thinking mind. We don't know what is in there. So how do we even begin to change it?

There are multitudes of products out there about the Law of Attraction and how to make it work for you. Each of those products has a different technique of cracking your subconscious mind, each one promising you the abundance and freedom you desire.

In reality, making the law of attraction work requires effort. The law of attraction is not a shortcut to success. It requires diligence and practice and in my opinion, requires re-programming of some core beliefs.

I've seen the law of attraction work on small test runs. When I first read about the law of attraction, the guru teaching recommended trying it on small things like attracting the perfect parking spot. I've tried this and it doesn't always work, but when it does, it's great to see in action.

I've learned that it works best when I'm in sync with the Universe. When I'm in alignment with the flow of the Universe, I can feel it. I feel good and I can make the law of attraction work. These are the types of days when nothing can go wrong for me. It's like the world is handing me everything, but unfortunately, not all my days are like this. I haven't found a consistent way to make the Law of Attraction work for me... yet.

The law of attraction works best when a person is mostly in a state of positivity and of alignment. This takes work, especially for those of us who are still learning and evolving. The key is practice. Practice positivity. Practice is the chisel that will chip away at your subconscious and allow it to begin changing and evolving.

Practicing to be positive is a great attitude to have--regardless if it can make the law of attraction work or not. Being positive will reap its own rewards and make for a more graceful way of living.

Here's my tip--if you can't make the law of attraction work for you, don't worry. Many people spend thousands of dollars on products and services trying to make this law work for them with little to no success. Practice having a positive attitude instead-- it's free and will make you feel good. Practicing positivity will shift your focus and energy to appreciating what you have rather than focusing on what you want or the things that you want to attract.

Having is easier than wanting.

Past Lives

This is the very first area of spirituality that I looked into. It was shortly after my dad died and I was looking for something to put my mind and my heart at ease. I could not accept that my dad was gone. I come from a superstitious culture and I started thinking about all the stories that my family would share, about souls remaining on earth for forty (40) days after death.

Stories about how family members would be visited by a loved one just before that loved one's passing—like the dream I had about my dad. After my dad passed, my mom confided in me and my brother that she could still feel my dad's presence around her. She felt like my dad was watching over her.

I was thinking about all these things--about my dream, about my mom's feelings about my dad's presence, and about our family stories when I began wondering if there was any real substance to them. Was there a tangible basis for the stories and the feelings or were we just reeling from the loss of Dad? This was when I was led to information on past lives.

After reading and researching about past lives, I learned that we are eternal. Our energies, our Spirits continue, and go back to God. It is only our physical body that dies. Our bodies are only temporary shells to house our Spirit while we go through this life.

What I also found fascinating about past life studies is that many of the experts in this field are doctors of medicine or doctors of psychology. These are people of science who look for proof and evidence before accepting a phenomenon as fact.

What the experts have found from direct accounts of their patients are incredible. But it wasn't the fantastic nature of the stories that captured these doctors' attention; it was the consistency of the stories they were told.

Here's what the experts have discovered about past lives:

~Our natural embodiment is that of energy/Spirit. In Spirit form, we live in divinity.

~Our Spirit-self decides when there is a need to return to earth life. This need to return could be because there are more lessons to learn, or perhaps there is a purpose that needs fulfillment, or perhaps we are returning as part of a group. Whatever the reason might be, the choice to return is completely ours.

~Once this choice is made, our Spirit-self works with various phyla of the angels to prepare for our physical birth and return into this world.

~The Virtues help us by working with us to plan out our life chart. It is these angels that assist us with mapping out the course of our lives in accordance with the reasons we have for returning. The life chart plots out events in our life that will lead us to the lessons we want to learn. The life chart begins with our birth. We decide when we are born and to which parents. The life chart progresses from birth all the way to our death.

~The Dominions review the deeds we have done from our other past lives. This review is designed to help us gain knowledge from those past lives. This can be considered a type of schooling that our Spirit-self must complete before being given the ok to come back to earth.

~The Dominions help to educate our Spirit by accessing the Akashic Records. The Akashic Records are basically the equivalent of a library. Only this library is none like we would ever see or experience in this world. The information stored within the Akashic Records is completely about us! These records contain every action, every deed, and every thought we have ever made. The rule of thumb applied to the Akashic Records is "as above, so below." This means that whatever we do down here, gets recorded up there--equal and proportional. As you create your thoughts, your thoughts' energy frequency flow into the ethers of heaven and into the Universal Consciousness and starts getting recorded within the book of You. Every single person has an Akashic Record that reveals that person's entire history--past, present, and yes, future. (Time and space are relative, but this is a whole other discussion.)

~Once the preparation is done and we are ready to start our new earth life, we are given additional help through the constant vigilance of our guardian angels. Our guardian angels are with us from the time we are born to the time we pass over. Our guardian angels do their best to keep us on our life path. If we stray, our guardian angels can call-in extra help to get us back on track.

~Once we enter into our physical body and are born back into earth life as a newborn babe, we forget about our Spirit origins and we begin to live as physical beings rather than spiritual ones.

This cycle continues so long as our Spirit-self chooses to be re-born into the physical world. Each life will be different and each life will produce different lessons.

In our physical life, the people that come into our lives are part of our spirit family group. These are members of our celestial family that also chose to come back. The appearance of people in our lives is of no coincidence. According to past life experts, everyone that comes into our life has a purpose for arriving, for leaving, and for doing what they do. Many times, it is because there is a lesson attached to that particular person and the specific events that they bring about.

For example, do you have somebody in your life right now that you absolutely cannot stand? This person is likely someone from your spirit family who agreed to come back with you to help you with a lesson you wanted to learn. The role that they happen to agree to play in your physical life is of someone you dislike with a passion. Can you imagine the commitment this Spirit has to you to take on this role?

If there is someone in your life that causes you severe emotional reaction; think about stepping outside of your situation for a moment. Ask yourself some questions about this person. For example, what is it about your relationship with this person that makes you feel the way you do? Why do you have such a strong reaction to this person? Strong feelings whether positive or negative have a source and a reason. Are you learning any lessons from this person? Be honest now. Is there something more about this person that you have not discovered that could change your perspective? Would you be willing to make that discovery? Why or why not?

Past life history or memory can continue to affect us in our current life. Issues or trauma that we were not able to resolve during a specific lifetime can manifest itself in our current life. Who knows how many lifetimes each of us has lived? What did we do in those lives? Ever wonder if you've been royalty in a past life? A cherished leader? Maybe a soldier or a scorned lover? Perhaps a Franciscan Monk? How many times have you lived as a man, as a woman? Have you ever died as a child? Which of these past lives is having the most effect on your current life? Why?

We may not remember past life memories, but these memories are with us--stored in our very cells. It is within our DNA. However, these past life memories are not easily accessible. Yes, there are those with gifts or intuitive talent that can tap into this wellspring of information. However, for most of us, these memories are blocked. At least the memories remain blocked until some event triggers a spontaneous release of a particular past life memory. And even then, we would not understand where the memory is coming from.

Understanding your past life history could be priceless in understanding your current blocks or challenges. It may be that your current struggles are not necessarily the result of things you've done in this life, but rather the manifestation of problems that have followed you throughout all of your lifetimes--that you are somehow re-living those issues over and over again, until you are able to conquer those issues and change the path of your current life and also the path of your future lives.

For some, the notion of past lives and the theories that go behind it can be upsetting. Does it mean that our lives are predestined and that we don't have a choice? Does it mean we cannot get out of a bad situation because we were meant to live that experience? My opinion on the matter is this: yes, I do believe that to some extent, our lives are mapped out and there are certain points in our lives when we are meant to experience an event and gain lessons from that event--both good and bad. However, do I think we are stuck in our life? No I don't, not at all.

God equipped us with free will. This very powerful tool gives us the ability to make choices or not make choices. Remember that your free will is sacred. God, the angels, the spirit guides-- they will not interfere with our free will. The priceless gift of choice is for us to make.

I believe that although we may be presented with certain situations and events that we have to experience, how those situations pan out will depend on how we choose. I believe this is why the angels go through the trouble of schooling us and reviewing our Akashic Records with us before we are born. We learn from our past. We know what mistakes we've made and we know what successes we've accomplished and this knowledge can continue to help us in this life.

You might be saying, but Mignon, we don't remember our past lives. You are absolutely correct. We, as in our physical selves don't remember, but our Spirit does. We have everything within us to become the person we are meant to be. Remember intuition? That is Spirit trying to guide you. Do you listen or do you ignore the whisper?

If you choose to ignore the whisper of your Spirit, I believe your Spirit will start to get restless and will ask, then demand, an awakening. This calling comes when we have wandered too far from our intended life and our Spirit knows it.

You are reading this book, which tells me you have chosen to answer the call, but there will be many who won't. That is ok too. There is no negative judgment from God. Not waking up doesn't mean a person is any less worthy or any less divine.

That person is simply not ready. That's all it is. Eventually, the calling will fade and they will continue with their day-to-day life.

They will have another opportunity, if they choose, to gain the lessons they intended--in another life. Do overs are ok.

I am thankful to have found this area of study. The belief that we are eternal rings true in my heart. That we don't stop existing when we take our last breath is peaceful to me. After reading and accepting that the concept of past lives is part of our divine cycle, my dad's passing became easier for me to bear. I began to understand, that yes, his physical embodiment is gone, but he is present. His Spirit survives and continues to be a part of our life. He is still there--just in different form.

My dad returned to his true nature and returned back to God. Most of all, I now understand that by returning to God, my dad is no longer suffering. He is no longer in pain, and he is surrounded by the kind of love that can only be experienced in the presence of our Creator. My dad is free and he is whole again.

Spirit Guides

We have many helpers to assist us in our journey. We have the angels and we also have Spirit Guides. Spirit Guides are different from angels in that Guides once lived as a person like you and me.

Guides understand the trials and challenges that we go through as people. Guides understand human drama because they once lived in it as well. Guides may be better (at times than angels) in helping us figure out our issues and leading us to creative answers because they understand the complications of earthly life.

Spirit Guides can be Ascended Masters or members of our spirit family group. Guides come into our lives depending on what we need at certain junctures of our lives. Spirit Guides may also show up for a very specific task and leave once that task is completed. For example, when our guardian angels need some extra help to get us back on track. They may call on one of our spirit guides to lend some assistance and help us see the light. Like our angels, our guides are there to give us support and help; and just like our angels, our guides do not interfere with our free will.

You may find that you are more connected with either your angels or your guides. There is sometimes a natural preference as to which group you lean towards. That is totally ok. I tend to call on my angels more, but I am making it a point to get to know my guides and to build a stronger connection with them. Much like our angels, our guides are also our best friends in waiting. They are there to help us and only want the very best for us.

This is the end of this section and I hope I have sparked your interest in one or more of these subjects.

***Here's my tip*--**as your knowledge grows and expands, so will your desire to share what you've learned. I encourage you to keep learning because there is always more waiting to be discovered in this journey. However, keep in mind that not everyone you meet will be open and accepting to what you have to share. Each person's journey is different and we have to allow for each person to find their own way and in their own time. So my advice to you is: be like the angels who stand by our sides. Offer your knowledge and wisdom when asked. When not asked, live your words through your actions. Act out your inner divinity by being an example of love and kindness--actions speak louder than words.

Chapter 5: Tools and Practices

Practice of Breathing

Breathing is a lost art. Breathing should be so natural and effortless, yet I've learned that many of us do not breathe correctly. Because of our harried lives we often take short shallow breaths. At times we even hold our breaths unconsciously. Yet, taking deep breaths can be one of the most cleansing and relaxing practices to have.

As you read this passage; become aware of your breathing. Take a deep, slow breath in through your nose. Feel the air fill up your lungs. Don't be afraid to let your belly expand. When your lungs feel full, slowly release the air through your nose. Feel the air leaving through your nostrils. Take another deep inhale.

Close your eyes as you fill up your lungs with that cleansing breath. When you are ready, slowly exhale and imagine all your tension leaving you. You've released your tension with the release of your breath. Do these slow inhalation and exhalation five times. Take your time with this.

How do you feel? Feels pretty good doesn't it? Apply this practice whenever you can. When you are at work and have a few minutes, this practice is great at letting go of some your stresses.

Having a tough day in general? Find a quiet place, do the breathing exercise and listen. Listen intently to your breaths. It is calming and will help you center so you can get back to life in a more grounded state.

Focusing on the act of breathing clears the mind of all daily distractions and clears our energy, enabling us to better connect with the Spirit within.

~Anon

Attitude of Gratitude

Find your blessings and give your thanks. This may be difficult if you find yourself carrying the burdens of life. I know I've been there, but please believe that it will get better.

You have a say in this and you can help make things better by simply giving thanks. Choose gratitude. Finding your blessings and giving thanks shifts your perception. It shifts your energy and your attitude towards the positive. Being in a positive state will bring about positive results.

Remember I mentioned earlier that having is easier than wanting? Let's think about this for a moment. When you want something, don't you feel some level of stress and anxiety? The feelings may be slight, but it's there. Now, think about all the stuff you already have—the people, the opportunities, and the things. Those are all blessings. Now notice your feelings. When you appreciate the gifts that you already have, the feelings you have are calm, peaceful, and joyous.

Before you go to sleep tonight, find ten (10) things to be grateful for. If you can't find ten (10), then find five (5). The lesson here is to find tangible things that you cannot deny. Don't make stuff up. This has to be real. You can start with the obvious things like your ability to read, your desire to learn, your need to grow, and your love of family and friends, etc. The more you practice being grateful, the more you will find your list expanding. That's how you know that your attitude of gratitude is working. Being thankful becomes easy and effortless.

For each new morning with its light, for rest and shelter of the night, for health and food, for love and friends, for everything Thy goodness sends.

~Ralph Waldo Emerson

Body, Heart, and Mind Awareness

Pay attention. Find those moments in between the mental chatter to find that quiet space and gain awareness of You. Don't be afraid to sit quietly and listen to what is in your mind and what your body is doing.

Having an awareness of You is essential to your ability to navigate this journey. Your awareness will lead to understanding. Awareness will allow you to discern between what your Spirit is sharing with you versus what your own old thought patterns are trying to maintain.

Let's focus on the body first. You can perform a quick self-check from head to toe, to feel what is going on with your entire body. Gain an awareness of your physical body. How do you engage your environment? Which of your basic five senses do you utilize the most—seeing, hearing, taste, smell, or touch? What about your sixth sense? Is that sense alerting you to any information? How does your body react to certain events and experiences? Do you get the tingles when certain ideas come into your head? Do you see colors or flashes of light when you close your eyes to meditate? Those are all signs of connection to Spirit.

Try this exercise:

Find a quiet place where you can sit and be comfortable. Once you find that comfortable spot sit back and listen to your environment. What do you hear? Do you hear noises from the outside? Are there birds chirping, dogs barking? Do you hear the machinery of your home buzzing and humming as they work to keep you comfortable? Can you hear yourself breathing?

As you listen to the different sounds around you, how is it making you feel? Pay attention to how your body is reacting. Are you becoming more relaxed as you sit still or perhaps you are becoming anxious because you cannot sit still for too long? What is your mind telling you to do? Does your mind's instruction sit well with your heart desires? How is this making you feel?

Do a quick check from head to toe. Start at the top of your head. How does your head feel? Does your head feel heavy? Are you holding your head straight or are you slumped over? What about your shoulders? Are they tight with tension or are they loose and relaxed? Check on your torso, your hips, thighs, legs, and feet. Do your lower limbs feel strong and stable? Do you have your feet firmly planted on the floor or do you have them resting on a table or ottoman? Are your toes relaxed or are they wiggling?

Do you feel like stretching? Does your body feel open or are you compressed into a ball? Have you checked your insides? How does your heart feel? Do you feel your heart beating loud and strong? What about your lungs? Can you feel your breath fill every corner of your lungs? Can you feel your chest expand as you inhale? How are your guts? Can you hear them gurgling and churching? Are your guts signaling you to eat or have you eaten too much?

Doing this exercise allows you to get in touch with all the hard working parts of your physical body. Although the goal is to gain a better understanding of the internal spiritual self, it is also important to take care of and understand the physical body. It is our body that will signal us first when there is something that warrants our focus and attention.

Let me give you an example. Have you been inspired by something you saw or heard? Didn't you feel excited? Your heart raced and you felt exhilarated about the idea. You were energized! If your body did not react in this way, you would not have known that you felt excited. That you felt good! This is the body's way of telling you that you were on to something incredible and significant, and this inspiration would be worth exploring.

Next, I want to take a moment to emphasize the importance of paying attention to your heart. Our heart is where we feel our emotions. Our heart is the vessel that our Spirit uses to communicate to us. Our Spirit lives in our heart. Love lives in our heart. The heart has its own intelligence. Our feelings are so incredibly strong and it is our heart that communicates all those feelings to us.

In this day and age of technology, it is very easy to be too cerebral, to be super analytical, and have too much in our heads. There is so much information, stimulus, and options that we have to process on a daily basis, that we often forget about our heart. We take for granted that the heart is also a guiding force to our wholeness. Our heart knows when something is right. We feel it and it makes us feel good. When our heart sings because of the joy it feels--we feel expanded, alive, and light. That's your Spirit talking through your heart. Listen. Feel. Pay attention.

How about awareness of our minds? This practice requires slowing down and removing yourself or distancing yourself from your mind chatter or more significantly removing yourself from your very own belief system. Our belief system is what we've acquired through our life experiences from the time we were babies to now.

Our belief system talks through our ego. I'll talk more about the ego later, but the voice you hear in your head that cause you to doubt yourself--that's the ego. Our minds are powerful and we believe what our mind tells us. But our minds lie and this untruth result in a tweaked perception of reality.

Part of this twisted perception is because of the judgments we place on a situation. Let me give you an example. I have had to work really hard on my issues with jealousy. When my husband and I were first married, I got very insecure whenever he would interact with other women. I would look at the other women and see how much prettier they were and how much more accomplished they were. I would notice how much my husband would smile around other women or how much he appeared to be enjoying their company. I would start thinking about how my husband was not like that with me. He certainly didn't give me that same kind of smile and he barely noticed I was around!

This was all very real to me, and how I described it here was exactly how I perceived it then. This caused me so much mental and emotional anguish, I was sure that my husband would leave me for one of these women. I kept questioning how my husband could stay with me when there were these other women who would probably make a better wife for him. They were prettier, sexier, smarter, blah, blah, blah, blah, blah. I saw things in his interactions that kept adding to my insecurities. My jealousy-monster was growing. Inevitably I created my own reality and my husband did leave. Not because he wanted to be with another woman, but because he could no longer endure the prosecution I kept putting him through.

It took a two year separation for me to realize that everything I saw and believed was all in my head. My mind was so convinced of the reality it had created that I could not see or believe anything else. Before my husband and I separated, he tried to talk to me repeatedly, but I wouldn't hear it. In my mind, he was making excuses to cover up his wrongdoing. He couldn't win, but in the end it was me who ultimately lost.

Oddly enough, our two year separation was probably the best thing that could have happened. I needed the distance and time away to figure out what was real. I began to understand that although our relationship at the time was not perfect, the issues that tore us apart only existed in my head.

Thank goodness my husband and I managed to reunite and we remain married to this day. My green eyed monster is no longer the destructive, ravenous beast bent on destroying our relationship. Yes, I still have my bouts of doubt, but it no longer possesses me like it used to. I am aware when the monster tries to rear its ugly head and I am able to tame it and send it on its way because I have learned to discern.

By becoming aware of my thoughts and taking the time to really separate myself from what is going on, I have been able to see more clearly and make better decisions. When I take the time to step back, I make it a point to take in the events happening around me. I do not assign a judgment and I simply observe.

Removing judgment from what you are observing allows you to better see things that are happening for exactly what it is. This could be applied to something as common as someone judging another because of the way the other person looked at them.

The person making the judgment call is only relying on their own perception and is not aware of everything else that could be happening with the looker. Could it be that the looker had a frown on their face because they were worried about something and just happened to look over in the other person's direction? In most cases, these are two strangers simply passing each other, but because of how one person perceives the other's action, one person could be completely offended; when in reality nothing happened.

I guess the point I'm trying to make here is that just because you think something is going on, it doesn't necessarily mean it is. Become aware. Heighten your perception.

Once you become more aware of the workings of your mind, you will be able to separate yourself from the situation and know when it is your ego that you are hearing versus when you might be thinking and processing a thought. Please understand that our thoughts are not bad, we need to think to live our daily lives. Thinking is how we function and perform the most basic of things like paying for our groceries or answering the phone. Thinking thoughts are not the same as ego based thoughts.

My warning comes when your thoughts become negative. When your thoughts make you doubt yourself, when your thoughts make you feel bad and unworthy. That is when you need to kick your awareness into gear and ask yourself, "what is going on *(insert your name here)*?!" Ask yourself if your thoughts are serving your greater good? If the answer is no, then it is not your Spirit that is talking to you. That's your own self-created monster that is trying to scare you into conformity.

Watch, listen, slow down, and pay attention to how your body, heart and mind are reacting to your situation at hand. Are they aligned with each other? In other words, is there cohesion between your body, mind, and heart? Are you in balance?

If you are feeling or thinking any sort of negativity or conflict, slow down even more and ask yourself, "why?" Try and figure out where that conflict is coming from. Is the doubt coming from your mind, your heart, or your body? Part of gaining awareness is to ask questions--lots and lots of questions. Questions allow you to expand. Questions shift your focus and energy.

Use the strength of your mind to your advantage. Did you know that our minds are naturally inclined to find answers?

When you change your approach to asking questions rather than making statements, your mind will automatically go in search of a solution. Your mind is the most powerful computer in the world after all. The speed of your thought cannot be matched by any artificial intelligence.

If by chance the answer you get is "I don't know why," that's ok too. You may not know why you are feeling discord at that moment. Be patient, it will come to you. Your question has been transmitted and the Universe will reveal the answer.

Here's an example. Feel the difference in these two passages. Read and reflect how your mind, body, and heart processes each verse.

"I feel tired."

"Why do I feel tired?"

Can you feel how you reacted to these two very simple passages? See how you are becoming more aware already!

Here's my tip--awareness, in my opinion, is one of the most important abilities you will need to learn and use on this journey. Awareness of your feelings, thoughts, and of your intuitions will connect you with your inner Spirit. As you grow and expand, you may feel like you're living in two worlds--our physical world and the world of Spirit. It is through your awareness that you will be able to balance and navigate both these worlds and blend them seamlessly.

Angel Cards

Angel Cards are my favorite tool of all. Angel cards are a deck of cards illustrated with images of different angels. Each card offers a message. There are different spreads you can use depending on what your question may be. The combination of the cards along with the messages on each card is how an answer or response is provided.

I read my cards at least once a week for various reasons. If I am confused or unsure about an issue, I consult with my cards to give me guidance. If I am frustrated about a challenging situation, I consult my Angel Cards to give me clarity. Mostly, I read my cards because I am interested in hearing general guidance from my angels.

Because I cannot hear or see into the spiritual realm, I need help in communicating with the angels. The cards allow me to *hear and see* the angels' messages. I find that the cards provide gentle guidance and advice. It doesn't ever feel forceful or intrusive. There is also wisdom in the cards that you can feel being shared.

Although I pull my cards on a regular basis, I do not rely on my cards to make my decisions.

Angel cards are not meant to replace our judgment. Rather, the cards are there to provide more information, advice, and guidance that can be used in the decision making process.

Angel cards are aligned with your energy and are surprisingly accurate in reflecting back what you might be feeling--even the feelings you might be denying. I have had my cards for several years I am more connected with my cards now, in comparison to when they were brand new.

For fun, I wanted to pull a card for this section so that you can have an angel's message as you read. This message is from *Doreen Virtue's Archangel Oracle Cards*:

Notice the loving guidance you hear inside your mind, or from other people. You're hearing true Divine guidance very clearly. It comes in the form of repetitious messages, urging you to improve a situation for yourself or others. Pay close attention to everything you hear in your mind and with your physical ears. Divine directives are repetitious, loving, and to the point. Ask me for help if you need clarification on anything you hear.

~ Archangel Zadkiel

Remember the angels are there for you. Call on them whenever you need. If you are like me and don't have the gifts of clairaudience or clairvoyance (clear hearing or clear seeing), the cards may be great tool for you to *hear or see* your angels' messages.

Reiki

Reiki is a form of energy healing technique developed in Japan in the 1920's. The principle behind Reiki is working with both

Universal energy as well as the person's life force/energy to bring about whole person wellness.

Reiki is non-invasive. It is gentle and very relaxing. The interesting thing is that the method used by Reiki practitioners is called "laying of hands," however, in the sessions I've had, my practitioner does not touch me.

My session started out with me getting in a comfortable supine position. My practitioner reminded me not to cross my arms or legs. I took three deep breaths, closed my eyes, and she got started. I could tell where my practitioner was moving and where she was positioned around the table. I could hear the rustle of her clothe and the sound of her steps, but I don't feel her touch me.

During the session, I felt myself get very relaxed. My body began to feel heavy and my breathing evened out. As the session progressed, I started to feel waves and swirls and pulling of energy around parts of my body that my practitioner was working on. The feelings were not unnerving, although it was different from anything that you or I would experience under normal circumstances. The feel of the energy, at times felt very euphoric.

Reiki practitioners are very cognizant of energies and can incorporate their work to heal the chakras. Remember the chakras are our very own strong hold of energy and if they are not functioning properly it could mean that we suffer with physical, emotional, mental, and/or spiritual ailments. Because a Reiki practitioner understands the forces of energy as it relates to both the Universe and our bodies, they are able to assist in our healing by moving or clearing these energies through our body and our chakras.

My very first Reiki session was incredible. It was during this session that I had my one and only experience of a vision (outside of dreaming). In addition, and this is what floored me even more than having a vision, is that I felt hands! You might be thinking it was probably my practitioner. I can, without a doubt, tell you that it wasn't my practitioner. At the time I felt the hands on me, my practitioner was standing at the front end of the table where my head was.

I could feel her and hear her directly behind my head. I felt the hands on top of my stomach with the direction of the hands coming from my left side. The pressure I felt from the hands was steady, gentle, and warm. I was not frightened or alarmed. I actually had the urge to place my hands on top of *the hands* because the sensation was so comforting, but I wasn't supposed to move and I didn't want to do anything that would disrupt this amazing experience I was having. I wanted it to continue.

I talked with my practitioner after this session and she explained that many times she receives assistance from Spirit Guides and Angels during a session to help with her client's healing. I was thankful for all the help. Not only did I receive physical healing during my session, but more importantly it really opened my eyes to the world of Spirit. It validated for me that there is absolutely more, beyond our physical world. I had a very concrete experience that I could not deny.

Meditation

I mentioned earlier that I struggle with meditating because of my constant mind chatter. Over the years, I've retreated and have learned to live in my head. Quieting my mind is extremely difficult; however, I have not given up and am continuing to pursue this. Why, you ask?

Because attaining that space of quiet is extremely important in having the ability to hear your inner Spirit. It is within this space of quiet where we gain clarity, perspective, and divine guidance and just like you I am in pursuit of my truth. By quieting our mind we open ourselves to the Universe.

Guided meditation seems to work best for me. I can listen intently to the voice and put my entire focus on the directions being given to me by the narrator. Having guidance is helpful in providing the cues for the imagery or the landscapes that the meditation will take you through.

Another helpful type of meditation is a breathing meditation. Instead of having a narrator; you are listening and focusing on your breaths. I can do a breathing meditation, but only for a short few minutes because I end up falling asleep! It's quite relaxing.

This may seem obvious, but I'll alert you to it anyway. Whenever possible, try to meditate in a comfortable sitting position. By sitting up, your body has to remain "alert" so that it can continue to hold you upright. This will help with preventing sleepy spells.

If you are like me and have difficulty quieting your mind, try guided meditation or meditating to music. This will give you a source of focus and will reduce or even eliminate your mind chatter. In addition, give yourself a break. Don't put the added pressure on yourself to meditate for extended periods of time. The goal is to get better with each practice. Gurus and masters spend years perfecting this craft. For us beginners, a few minutes at a time is great.

Our minds are busy places and quieting it takes some effort. If at first you can only quiet your mind for one minute--feel good about that. Give yourself a minute every day to meditate. When this starts to feel more natural, increase your time to two minutes and continue to gradually increase from there. How fast and how often you increase your meditating time is up to you. The important thing is to practice and to find space in your day to allow this quiet time to happen.

Meditation here may think down hours to moments. Here the heart may give a useful lesson to the head and learning wiser grow without his books.

~William Cowper

Prayer

Did you know that prayer is a form of meditation? I didn't and was pleasantly surprised when I found out that it was.

While I was growing up, the prayers that I learned through the church were very formal. The prayers were in the form of verses and even the way they were recited had a certain tone to it. I could always tell what prayer was being spoken just by the cadence that the prayer took on.

My prayers are not so rigorous. My prayer time is my time with God and I choose to spend my time with less formality. What I find important is that my focus and attention is on God and taking the time to reflect upon the experiences and lessons I am being provided. My prayer time allows me time to give thanks, ask for clarity, ask for support or to simply just converse with God.

However you choose to pray, make it your own and make it special to you. There are lots of forms of prayer. If chanting a prayer, Gregorian Monk style, is your way, then embrace it and chant away. Feel the power that a chant can deliver to your soul.

If singing your praises is your form of prayer, sing with all your heart and feel the voice of God flow through you and your song. If the traditional form of prayer is more your style, feel the verses of your prayer resonate through your Spirit.

It doesn't matter how you pray. What matters is that you take the time to connect and move towards the divine through your prayer.

In prayer it is better to have a heart without words than words without a heart.

~John Bunyan

Visualization

Visualization is an important component to many practices that will allow you better connection with your Spirit. Remember when you were a little kid and your imagination was endless? Your child mind could conjure up the most fantastic stories with the most colorful and impressive characters. This child mind is what you will tap into, when you do your visualization exercises. Your child mind knows no limits.

Visualization is fun. If you're thinking that your imagination is gone and it is hard for you to visualize--it's not. If you can daydream, you can visualize.

Let's try something. Let me ask you a question. What did you eat today?

When you read this question, didn't you automatically replay your day to remember what you've eaten? And when your mind got to the point in time when you were eating, didn't you get a picture of what you ate?

If I asked you to describe to me the first thing you remember eating today, I have no doubt that you would be able to describe to me exactly what you ate. When you remembered what you ate--you visualized!

Have fun with this. There are no limits where your imagination can take you. If you have an affinity towards being clairvoyant, visualization exercises are a great way to develop your talent. Trust what you see and trust how your feelings are guiding you with regards to that vision.

Let's try something else. Red Ferrari!

What flashed in your mind's eye? You saw what you know to be a red Ferrari. Can you tell me which way the car is facing? Can you tell me if the doors were opened or closed? Are there any emblems on the car? Now imagine yourself in the car. Are you behind the wheel in the driver's seat or are you riding shotgun? What are you doing while in the car?

How did you do? I bet it was pretty easy to see the red Ferrari. It is such an iconic car and very distinguishable. How did you do with placing yourself inside the car?

Practicing visualization will help you with your meditations, affirmations, and realizing your potential. If you can imagine it, you can make it happen.

I'm sure you've heard that top athletes often visualize themselves running through their course from start to finish. Labs have done tests on this visualization practice and have found that when an athlete visualizes themselves running a course (regardless of the sport) that the athlete's muscles and other body functions respond the same way as if the athlete was actually going through the course.

Our minds do not know the difference between real or imagined.

Visualize positive images. Visualize positive events. Visualize happy thoughts. Visualize the impossible and reach for the stars. Isn't part of this journey to find your true potential? Your Spirit knows what that potential is and your Spirit will communicate with you through your visualizations. Trust it. Aspire for it and it will come true. Our minds don't know the difference. Our bodies will live the experience as if the vision is real!

To accomplish great things we must first dream, then visualize, then plan... believe... act!

~Alfred A. Montapert

Journaling

Essentially your journal is where you capture your thoughts on paper. There are lots of ways to journal. There is the general journal where you write everything that is going through your mind. This is the old-fashioned version of the blog! In this type of journaling, you could write down your fears, your hopes, your dreams, or perhaps the memorable parts of your day that you want to treasure on paper.

There are also more specific types of journaling when you want to focus your collection of thoughts on a certain topic. For example a dream journal is where you would record your dreams and the dream symbols you remember. This is also where you could work out your interpretations and analysis of your dreams.

You could have an angel journal where you could record your thoughts, conversations, inspirations, and messages that you receive from angels. This would also be a great place where you could angel write.

No matter what type of journal you keep, I would recommend that when you are writing down your thoughts, that you do not censor yourself. Write down what comes to you--freely. Do not worry about how your handwriting looks or whether you are punctuating correctly. Do not edit things. Let your creativity and emotions pour out of you without a stopper.

When you return to these passages at a later time, you will see the honesty of your Spirit's message. You will gain clarity. You will see patterns. You will begin to ask questions of yourself and you can begin to find the answers.

In my opinion, the best way, a journal can help is by collecting your thoughts and emotions and acting as a repository. Journals help us by giving us a place to release and safely secure our most personal experiences.

For me, I've written in journals on and off throughout my life. While most people hang on to their journals for years, I shred mine after some time. In my earlier years, the call to journal only came when I was having trouble in my life. Most of my earlier journals had been a torrent of negativity and confusion-- especially in my teenage years.

No one is immune to teenage drama. My journals were my only outlet to release what I felt and what I thought. I don't want to hold on to negative memories. I got through those phases of my life and I managed to keep moving ahead. Shredding those journals was an extra step for me to release the negativity I captured. I could have probably burned my journals too; it surely would have had a more dramatic effect, but since I'm a bit of a klutz I didn't want to take a chance of causing a major fire.

Blocking

Blocking is really important if you are especially sensitive to other people's energy. Blocking is a way to protect you from being affected by negative energy or too much energy. For example, is there someone you work with who is a bit of a downer? When that person spends time with you, do you feel drained? Do you feel tired all of a sudden? How about when you go to a busy public place like a mall? Do you feel frazzled after your excursion? Do people with problems gravitate to you and want to pour their issues out to you?

This could mean that you are highly sensitive to energies. The reason you feel so exhausted when you are around a lot of people is because you are taking in some of those outside energies which is overloading you. To some extent those outside energies could even be taking over your own energy, which is why it could be difficult for you to separate your own positive energy from the negative ones that are overwhelming your system.

If you are sensitive you have to take care to protect yourself. I believe that people are natural empaths, so that we all naturally sense energy. However, there are those who are highly sensitive, like clairsentient intuitives. For those of you who are highly sensitive, more care must be taken in order to preserve your wellness—physically, mentally, emotionally, and spiritually.

Blocking takes practice and it is a practice that you should develop into a habit. Make it a part of your morning routine before you leave your home to greet the world. You never know who or what you will come across in your daily life and you always want to be prepared to meet all the different experiences that the world has to offer.

You could be faced with something as simple as having a friend who happens to be having a bad day. You are your friend's favorite sounding board, and because you are a wonderful, giving friend, you spend time with him or her, offering your support, and listening to their troubles. At the end of your visit with your friend, he or she is feeling much better. You however, feel very tired and all you want to do is go home, take a shower, and go to bed to end your day. Sound familiar?

My good friend is very sensitive to energies, especially when she started to realize her gifts. At first we could not figure out why her moods would turn dark. She would start feeling all sorts of aches and pains and at times get so sick for no apparent reason. These symptoms seemed random at first until we started talking about her episodes and realized that she always started to feel emotionally dark and physically ill whenever, she got around a certain group of people.

These people were not bad at all. In fact they were often called upon to help out in certain spiritual crisis situations. However, because of the type of work that they do and because of the intensity of the feelings and focus they have to generate to do their work, those mega-intense energies were throwing my friend completely off.

When we figured it out, a test of sorts came about. My friend began to politely excuse herself from invitations. We found that so long as she was not around these particular folks, that she stayed well and balanced, but if she spent any time with them even through social functions, she would get very sick.

Since realizing this, my friend has learned to block herself, or as she puts it 'close' herself off. There are different methods of blocking. One way is through visualization. Let's try this:

Imagine a white globe of light descending down from the heavens. The light is bright and illuminates everything around it as it descends down from the heavens. The light is filled with God's love and protection and you can feel the love radiating from the light.

As the white light reaches the top of your head or your crown chakra, allow the light to dissolve into your scalp. Feel the light travel down through your head and into your heart. Feel the warmth that surrounds you. When the light reaches your heart, the light and its rays begin to pulse and send out their brilliant beams outside of your body.

The rays begin to extend out and around, over and under you to form a protective bubble that is impenetrable by any negativity. Your bubble of white light becomes your armor or invisible shield so that you are not bombarded by lower vibrating energies as you go about your day. Your bubble preserves your own positive vibration and prevents you from feeling depleted.

My good friend's practice of blocking is more elaborate and she has found this method very effective for her. My friend gave me permission to share her technique and we hope that this is beneficial for you as well.

My friend is very connected to Archangel Michael. This powerful and very protective angel is a constant in her life. She calls upon Michael towards each of the holy directions of North, South, West and East. She uses blessed salt, oil, and holy water.

She places the salt under her tongue and she uses the blessed oil and water to make the sign-of-the-cross on her forehead and on her nape. While she is going through this ritual, she recites The Shema over and over again until she feels that she is well protected. My friend does admit that this is overkill, but having seen how sick she's gotten in the past, I can understand why she does not want to take chances with her blocking practice.

Just in case you are wondering what The Shema is, The Shema comes from Jewish traditions and is an affirmation and a declaration of faith in one God. Jewish traditions teach that The Shema is to be recited twice a day—once in the morning and once at night. This recitation is considered a divine commandment.

Last note on blocking, and this comes from practical observation of my friend's experiences. You have to find a happy balance with blocking. As my friend acknowledged her method is "overkill" and she recently learned that her methods are so effective that she completely closes herself off, that even her own energy cannot circulate.

My friend had a recent event she had to attend and because she anticipated that she would be around a lot of people, she took time to block herself using the method I described above. While she was at her event, she felt fine, but on her way home, she got terribly ill with a serious migraine.

We later saw our Reiki practitioner and our practitioner explained that all her energy got trapped in her system--especially around her third-eye, which also happened to be the center point of her migraine. My friend essentially created a pressure cooker effect by blocking too much. We learned that with blocking there has to be a healthy balance between protecting yourself from outside influences while still allowing your own natural energies to work and flow in and around you.

Release

Releasing is letting go of what is troubling you. This will explain it best:

> *Hakuna Matata! What a wonderful phrase*
>
> *Hakuna Matata! Ain't no passing craze*
>
> *It means no worries for the rest of your days*
>
> *It's our problem-free philosophy*
>
> *Hakuna Matata!*
>
> *~Simba, Timon, and Pumba*
>
> *(The Lion King)*

Release your worries and your fears, otherwise known as your blocks. Release the blocks that you are aware of. One of the ways to release is to bring awareness to a block.

Catch yourself in the middle of a "poor me" or "I can't do it" self-talk. Stop for a minute and ask yourself where that negativity is coming from? Your mind will seek out an answer. Capture the first thing that enters your mind. Remember that experience and see yourself again in that circumstance. Now that you have an awareness of where that block might be coming from, now you can release it!

Bring the vision back. Now instead of letting the vision play out like it normally does in your mind--change the ending or change the way you feel about the memory, change something that will make that recall a positive, rather than a negative experience. Infuse the memory with love and acceptance and then let it go. Yes, I know this seems crazy, but this is your story. If you change the energy of the memory, you change your present circumstance as well.

If you wish and want to give your spiritual release a physical ritual, perform some crazy gesture that symbolizes your release of that block. For example, I shred my journals. My friend likes to blow raspberries when she releases a block. It's funny to watch her. It is silly and it definitely makes her (and me) laugh, but that is the magic of it. Laughter is joyous, positive and full of high frequency energy. My friend definitely feels better after she raspberries her blocks away. I feel better after I shred my journals.

There are lots of release techniques that are available, but these are two of the more popular examples:

~Emotional Freedom Technique (EFT) Method or Tapping

~Sedona Release Method

If you don't know where your blocks are coming from, (and this is very common), enlist the assistance of a professional. Don't feel like you have to know how to do everything yourself.

You can receive healing from an energy healer who may be able to tap into a hidden block, or perhaps you can see an expert who can help you remember a past life. There are lots of choices. Choose the method and expert that feels right for you.

If you do decide to hire a professional, please, please do your research and listen to your Spirit's guidance to lead you to the appropriate person. Don't be afraid to make an initial phone call and ask questions about their services and philosophies.

You have to feel comfortable and safe about the person you will be working with. If you feel any kind of pressure or doubt about the service provider, pay attention to those feelings and don't second guess yourself. Trust your intuition. Your Spirit is sensing something about that person that is not right for you. Trust that the most appropriate person will be presented to you by Spirit.

This is the end of the Tools and Practices chapter. This is not an exhaustive list of the many practices and techniques that are out there. These are simply the ones that I have had personal experiences with and have found to be helpful in my daily life. I encourage you to do your own research to find the best approach that works for you.

Whether you choose to employ the tools and practices we reviewed in this book or you choose to find more of your own, know that the methods and techniques you use will be helpful in your ability to connect with your Spirit.

Here's my tip--you have been given an understanding or an explanation of different theories on Metaphysics in the previous chapter. Take that knowledge and combine it with a tool or practice to further strengthen your connection with Spirit. You'll find a combination that is just right for you. Trust your guidance and follow what feels right for you. For example, I use my understanding of angels, and I know that I have to ask for help to receive angelic assistance. So, I ask for the help I need and then I also read my angel cards to see if the angels have a message that could provide me additional information concerning my request.

Put into action what you learn. It is the only way you will know what works for you.

Without knowledge, action is useless and knowledge without action is futile.

~Abu Bakr

Chapter 6: Helpful Terms

In the early days of my journey, I often ran across terms that were commonly used but not defined. I reasoned that many of the authors must have felt that certain terms were so common in this field that everyone knew what they meant.

However, as a new seeker I was still learning the language. Although I could understand the gist of what was being said, I felt there was a lot that was lost on me. Needless to say I found this a tad bit annoying.

In an effort to save you time and hopefully some frustration, here is a list of terms that you will come across and may wonder about their meaning.

Flow--I'm sure you've heard of the saying "go with the flow." In our everyday world this saying takes on the meaning of 'hey relax and don't fight what's happening.'

In our spiritual world, flow is used in more general terms to reference the flow of the Universe, the flow of energy and the flow of Universal consciousness. Remember that everything is made of energy and that energy travels in waves and particles.

The flow is about what is happening within the Universe's matrix of energy. Energy is constant and always traveling--like water. By doing your practices and learning more about your inner Spirit you will achieve and you will get yourself in a state of being positive, open and receiving. You become attuned to the flow of the Universe. The Universe and all its gifts flow through you and with you.

When you're in the flow, everything happens like magic. You are relaxed and there is no resistance. So the next time someone tells you to go with the flow, it is advice well worth considering.

Violet Flames--the Violet Flames refer to a spiritual flame or light. There is significance in the color violet because violet is considered to have the highest vibratory frequency and is in concert with the highest etheric plane.

From a spiritual perspective the Violet Flame is about love, mercy, transformation, and alchemy. The Violet Flame is intelligence and love, and can assist us in our pursuit to discover our Spirit. When we discover who we are and we begin to find ourselves, we also naturally begin to transform and change.

The butterfly is a common symbol of this transformation. By finding our true self and discovering our Spirit, we break out of a binding cocoon to emerge as a bright, new, shining, physical-spirit. This transformation can be assisted by invocations of the Violet Flame.

I AM--the use of I AM is one of the most powerful statements you can use. It is derived from Exodus 3:14 when God said to Moses, *"I AM THAT I AM: and he said, Thus shalt thou say unto the children of Israel, I AM hath sent me unto you."*

This section basically comes from the time when Moses asked God what he needed to tell the people. God told Moses, tell them I AM that I AM. God's statement to Moses is that God IS and always will be. He is Presence and He is eternal.

If you prefer a more humorous version, Popeye the Sailor always used to say "I yam what I yam! Ach, ach, ach ach, ach (Popeye laughs)." In Popeye's context, he is fully and completely accepting of who and everything he is and proud of it.

When you use the I AM statement, you tap into your inner divinity and affirm for yourself that you are already everything that you are meant to be. Remember we are all children of God and His spark is in all of us. That is your I AM presence.

Go on declare it! Say it out loud! I AM *(your name here)* and I AM perfection.

If you feel like you are being conceited or boastful by declaring your perfection, let that negative feeling go. You are not being conceited or boastful. You are claiming your true self and as such simply stating fact. Enjoy it! It is who you are!

Ego--the ego is that part of our mind that has been raised, trained, and programmed by our life experiences from the time we were babies to now.

The Ego is often given a negative connotation because for the most part our ego uses fear and doubt as its tools to keep us planted and keep us stuck. Our ego is that part of our consciousness that is responsible for preserving and protecting us. The ego is not crazy about change and it does not like hurt and pain. Is the ego really bad? I don't think so. The ego is just doing what it knows to do.

The way our ego perceives the world is due to the experiences we've lived through in our lifetime. If we've had a lot of hurts in our life, our ego is going to be more wary and fearful of change. It will see change as a bad thing, something that can cause you emotional pain. But if we've had a pretty cush life and all of sudden we want to do something different that seems threatening to our cush life, the ego will also activate, because now something safe and stable is being disturbed for something unknown.

In the world of spirituality, the ego can be considered an obstacle to growth. Why you ask? Because the ego does not like change and growth means change. You have to change in order to grow--physically, emotionally, and spiritually.

The good news is that you can retrain the ego. It is part of how our mind works and our minds can be reprogrammed. Reprogramming takes time, patience, and diligence. It took years for us to be shaped into the person we are. Now that our current belief system and thought patterns are no longer working to serve us, it is time to change. You will have to be patient with yourself. It takes time to shape a new you.

You may even experience fluctuations in your growth and progress. Don't get frustrated if all of a sudden you feel like nothing is happening. Trust that God is always working. Sometimes that time of stillness is needed to let all the new information sink in and take root.

Channel--channeling is the process where someone connects with the spirit world for guidance.

A channel is a person who is able to connect with the world of spirit and give us back information obtained from the divine. A channel can give over their physical self to allow spirit to communicate. A channel may or may not be conscious of the messages that are being spoken through them while channeling. A channel can connect with non-physical beings like Angels, Spirit Guides, and Ascended Masters.

Medium--a medium is someone who can interface with the world of our ancestors. By ancestors, I mean our loved ones (family and friends) who have passed on. The passing could be recent or from a long time ago. How a medium interfaces with spirit depends on the medium's intuitive gift. They might connect through clairvoyance, clairaudience, or a combination of any of the "clair" abilities. A medium opens him or herself up completely to the world of spirit in order to receive the intended message for the family member.

Psychic--a psychic is a general term for someone who can glean information from the invisible world. Psychics use their sixth sense to read information from a person. The sixth sense consists of the "clair" abilities. This term can be used in place of an intuitive. A more modern term for psychic is **Intuitive Counselor**.

All mediums are psychics because all mediums use at least one "clair" ability to connect with those who have passed. A medium's "clair" ability just happens to be specialized in connecting with our loved ones who have passed on.

BUT, not all psychics are mediums, because not everyone who has a "clair" ability can connect with the dead. Again this is a specialized ability.

Blocks--Blocking is different from blocks. Blocking is the act of protecting yourself with a type of energy force field

A **block**--is an energetic issue that lives somewhere within our cells or our subconscious and is hindering us from being able to move forward. Most people have an issue that keeps coming up over and over again no matter what they do. For example, most people have a fear of success. Crazy, I know. Who would be afraid of being successful? Right?

I was, until I realized what I was doing. When I became aware, then I started to notice that whenever I set a goal for myself, I would often find a way to not complete my goal. I would self-sabotage before I could reach success. Why? I think it's because I was afraid of what success would do to me or how it might affect me--that it would change me as a person somehow. My fear of success was a huge block because it prevented me from expanding and from growing. It kept me stuck.

Chapter 7: Closing

Thank you for sticking with me through the end of this book. You are probably wondering "now what?"

Now you keep moving ahead in your journey with some solid information neatly tucked in your mind and hopefully in your heart.

The quest to find Spirit is ultimately about finding yourself. It's what people are talking about when they say "Be authentic." Finding your true self, the self you were meant to be according to God, is waiting to be found.

Pay attention to your instincts. Pay attention to how your body reacts when you are faced with certain decisions. Finding yourself is also about learning to trust you. Don't rely on other people's opinions--they are on a different journey and cannot truly understand what is right for you.

You are the master of you. Everything you need to discover who you truly are is already inside of you. Believe and trust that the path is being laid out for you and it is the journey itself that will ultimately shape you as a person.

If you started this journey because you were unhappy or felt like you were in a rut, you will begin to feel a true calmness that comes from within when you begin to understand and accept what you are truly about. Life will not seem so challenging. It will not feel like life is fighting you. In fact, even in the midst of challenges, you will continue to find blessings. Acknowledge those blessings and more will come.

Use the different practices we talked about to help you. Connect with the Universe through your Angels, your Guides, and through your very own intuitive talents. These resources are all meant to help and support you through this lifetime. You were not meant to go at this alone. God is good and just like any parent; He wants what is best for his children.

When my journey started, I had no idea where it would take me. All I knew was that I had to answer this undeniable call coming from within. This calling had whispered to me before, but I was able to easily ignore it. I had no understanding that the feelings of restlessness and the feeling that something was missing from my life was actually a call from my Spirit. The Universe was calling to me and I needed to answer. God/Universe/Source was not going to let up until I woke up.

I'm glad I took the red pill, and you will be too. Being on this journey has opened my eyes to a much different world. Nothing has changed in the physical world, except my perception of it. And that change has made a huge difference. I now see the miracles that are always around us. I appreciate the synchronicity of life and that there is always a divine plan at work. Although I don't know where my journey will take me, I am looking forward to the lessons I will gain from this odyssey.

My wish is for you to find yourself in a place of peace, fulfillment, and a place of understanding. May you unite once again with your Spirit and embrace your inner divinity.

I hope to continue to be of service to you by sharing more lessons along the way. I never would have guessed that I would pen a book, but perhaps this is a part of the path that my Spirit wanted to discover. What amazing possibilities are waiting for you?

Learn to get in touch with the silence within yourself, and know that everything in life has purpose. There are no mistakes, no coincidences, all events are blessings given to us to learn from.

~Elisabeth Kubler-Ross

Share Your Thoughts

Your thoughts and input are so important to me and to other seekers. If you enjoyed this book, please share your thoughts with others who are also on the journey. We learn best from each other.

Go to the link below to leave a review.

http://www.amazon.com/Spirit-101-Overview-Spirituality-ebook/dp/B00ACD88IQ/

Want more information? Come visit my blog at http://iggylife.com/

Check out the Downloads page to get a free report on Hatha Yoga. In this report I will provide an explanation of the importance of Yoga for your mind, body, and spirit connection as well as provide you gentle relaxation techniques through the practice of Hatha.

Let's connect on:

https://twitter.com/MignonSupnet

https://www.facebook.com/pages/Books-Blogs-Bits/345767795513819

I wish you bliss and abundance in all you do. Let your Spirit shine bright.

Thank you for your support!

CPSIA information can be obtained at www.ICGtesting.com
Printed in the USA
LVOW08s1815090914

403241LV00028B/946/P